Includes
Activities and
Exercises

MAXIMUM
Perfecting Student Grammar and Writing
IMPACT

Senior Editor
Paul Moliken

Editors
Darlene Gilmore
Stephanie Polukis

Reviewing Teachers
Deborah Ford
Anna J. Small Roseboro
Julie Seeley
Sarah Zeek
Mary Zirillo

Cover and Text Design
Maria J. Mendoza

Layout and Production:
Jeremy Clark

PRESTWICK HOUSE, INC.
"Everything for the English Classroom!"

ISBN: 978-60389-175-2

Introduction

Maximum Impact gives you a way to pinpoint common errors that many people make when they write. However, just understanding the errors is not much unless you can practice correcting them.

The book contains many chances for you to do just that, and your writing will surely improve once you understand many of the techniques to use in order to avoid these mistakes. Many of the exercises ask you to explain why one way of doing things is preferable to another. In these cases, we have given you reasons that you'll be able to apply to explain your changes. In other cases, there may be more than one way to correct a mistake. That's what is exciting about writing. No one *best* way exists for you to say some things. However, that does not mean your writing can't be improved. Revising your work, eliminating confusing parts and errors, and saying what you want to say as clearly as possible are three of the best ways to improve your writing.

The goal of *Maximum Impact* is to lead you through the process of shaping your writing—figuring out what you want to say, and then maximizing the effect of your words. Some of this will involve the correction of small, but important, things like punctuation marks, commonly confused words, and spelling errors.

This book assumes you already know terms like *verb, noun, phrase, clause, fragment, prepositional phrase, subject,* and *predicate*. While the terms are used throughout the book, the definitions and explanations of each term are not emphasized.

We're sure that, with practice, you will become a more accomplished writer.

Part I: Sentence Sense

Part II: Avoiding Ambiguity

Part III: Show You Know

Part IV: Commonly Confused Words

Table of Contents

Part V: Writing to Win

Cumulative Exercises

Activities for Improving Student Understanding

Part I:
Sentence Sense

In this section, you will learn how to avoid
common sentence errors like run-ons
and comma splices.

Chapter One

What makes a complete sentence?

You speak in sentences every day. A sentence expresses a complete thought, fact, or idea. For example, you might go up to your friend Jerod and say, "Lend me a dollar." That's one complete thought, and it's expressed in one sentence. Jerod's response to you might be a question: "Why should I?"

Independent vs. Dependent Clause

In order for you to know what a complete sentence looks like, you have to know what dependent and independent clauses are.

A **dependent clause** has a subject and a predicate, but it begins with a word that prevents the clause from ever standing alone (these words are called *subordinating conjunctions*). The following three examples are all dependent clauses, not sentences; the subordinating conjunctions are the first words in each example.

- because Sheila has six sisters
- unless you go to the dance with me
- after the police investigated

Try saying each one. Does any one of them sound like a complete sentence? NO. That's because the writer's thoughts are not complete. What about Sheila's sisters? What will happen if you don't go to the dance? What did the police find after the investigation?

An **independent clause**, just like a dependent one, has both a subject and a predicate. The difference is that an independent clause does not begin with a subordinating conjunction. It can stand on its own. It is a complete sentence.

The following are independent clauses:

- Mickey answered the phone.
- Airplanes and cars cut down travel time.
- That book with the ripped cover belongs to me.

When you read each of these, you understand what the writer is trying to say. Unlike the three dependent clauses, these do not leave you with questions about what is happening.

Now, look at the following sentence:

<u>If you want dessert,</u>   <u>you must ask for it politely</u>.
dependent clause   **independent clause**

This complete sentence consists of a dependent clause attached to an independent clause. The dependent clause is "If you want dessert." It begins with a subordinating conjunction—"if"— and it has a subject and predicate. However, "If you want dessert." isn't a completed thought. This clause cannot stand on its own as a sentence.

Test yourself: Say to someone, "If you want dessert," then stop. What do you think that person might do?

The second part of the sentence is an independent clause. It has a subject, "you," a predicate, "must ask for it politely," and no subordinating conjunction.

Test yourself: Say this part of the sentence aloud. Does it sound like a complete idea?

EXERCISE I:

Try to come up with five dependent clauses and five independent clauses. We have done two of each for you.

Answers will vary.

Dependent Examples	**Independent Examples**
Whenever Roberta wants	Roberta wants a pony.
If you ever catch me	I'll give you a dollar if you catch me.

Dependent Examples	Independent Examples
1. _____	1. _____
_____	_____
2. _____	2. _____
_____	_____
3. _____	3. _____
_____	_____
4. _____	4. _____
_____	_____
5. _____	5. _____
_____	_____

Remember: *A sentence can contain a dependent clause, as long as that*

(!) *clause is attached to an independent clause. If there is no independent clause, though, the sentence is not complete.*

Why do you need to know this?

Knowing the difference between dependent and independent clauses will help you understand why a sentence is considered complete or incomplete. This, in turn, will help you avoid writing *sentence fragments* (see page 14).

Come up with words that make each dependent clause into a sentence.

Teacher's Note: Explain that sentence variety will improve if these clauses do not always go at the beginning of students' sentences.

Answers will vary.

1. Once Jennifer had gone to the skating rink

2. Although I had read the book

3. So that all the campers could set up their tents

4. Unless you tell me the truth

5. While the pirate hid the treasure

6. If only the present were what I had wanted

7. Because of the fierce fire

8. Whenever the boss comes into the office

9. After the sky darkened

10. Although it was freezing

11. Unless there is enough fertilizer

12. Because Jazmine said so

13. Rather than playing with the kids

14. In order to change the lock on the house

15. Even though we had all the songs we could ever listen to for the rest of our lives

Chapter Two

Sentence-Ending Punctuation Marks:
Period, Question Mark, and Exclamation Point

In writing, as in speaking, you use sentences to get your ideas across. Because you can't speak to your reader with your own voice, you have to know how to write sentences so that your reader will understand you. If you're standing with Mark in the hallway of your school, he will know that your sentence has ended when you stop talking. But in your writing, you have to use a **punctuation mark** to show that a sentence is over.

You may use a **period** if the sentence is a simple statement that does not express strong emotion or ask a question. For example, the following sentences each end with a period:

- I think I have heard this song before.
- The medicine has some serious side effects.
- I just learned that Opal will be coming to the picnic.

A **question mark** goes at the end of a sentence that asks a question. This type is called an *interrogative* sentence, and it will sound as if it needs an answer.

- Is Sharon dancing?
- What time is it?
- I know who Jason's date was last night; do you?
- Where are those scissors that I lent you?

All of these four questions can be answered:

- Is Sharon dancing? *Yes, she is.*
- What time is it? *It's 4 o'clock.*
- I know who Jason's date was last night; do you? *No. I thought it was Laura.*
- Where are those scissors that I lent you? *I gave them to Helen.*

Some sentences sound as if they could be questions, but they are actually statements. Be careful not to put a question mark at the end of a sentence like this. Sentences that *seem* as if they need an answer, *but do not,* must have a period after them, not a question mark.

- I wonder if Sharon is dancing.
- I wish I knew what time it was.
- I knew who Jason's date was last night.
- Please tell me where those scissors are that I lent you.

Finally, an **exclamation point** goes at the end of a sentence that expresses a strong emotion like anger or surprise. These are called *imperative* sentences.

- Help!
- I can't believe he said that!
- Don't you dare pick up that phone!
- That was an awesome movie!

Don't forget to use a capital letter to begin a sentence. Look at the following pairs of sentences. Notice how each sentence begins with a capital letter. The capital letter is a sign that a new thought is starting.

- The election is coming up. There are signs everywhere.
- Liz hit a home run. Our team won the game.
- If our flight is cancelled, we'll be in big trouble. We don't have hotel reservations.

Put the proper punctuation marks at the end of the following sentences:

1. Do you know how many cars a billion dollars could buy **(?)**

2. I hate Halloween **(!) or (.)**

3. Stop that immediately **(!)**

4. My cousin Carlos called me yesterday, but he didn't talk much **(.)**

5. When was the game finally over **(?)**

6. My computer crashed for the tenth time today, and I'm really furious **(!) or (.)**

7. Why is the book under the table **(?)**

8. Why I studied for that test is a question I cannot answer **(.)**

9. Why should I stop working on my project **(?)**

10. Fred accidentally drove through the red light **(.)**

Chapter Three

Sentence Fragments

The sentence is the basic unit of thought in English, and it is going to be your most important tool as you put your ideas on paper for a reader to understand. The reader will know that when the sentence ends, one idea has ended, and a new idea is beginning. However, sometimes we write incomplete ideas down, but we think they are sentences.

You learned in the first chapter that a dependent clause alone does not make a complete sentence. In this chapter, we'll discuss incomplete sentences, which are called **fragments**. Fragments are trying to become sentences, but they are missing needed parts, like a subject or a predicate. You need to avoid fragments in your writing, and write in complete sentences.

Look at the following fragments. After each fragment is an explanation of what is wrong:

1. The balloon.

This sentence fragment has only a noun—"the balloon." We don't know if the balloon did something or something was done to the balloon. The fragment needs some kind of predicate. For instance, if you said, "Alfonso popped the balloon right next to my ear," you would have a complete idea and, therefore, a complete sentence.

2. Was caused by germs.

This fragment contains a predicate, but no subject. What was caused by the germs? Maybe the whole sentence is supposed to say, "Because the infection was caused by germs, we were able to treat it with medicine."

3. Beyond a doubt.

This fragment has no subject or predicate. You need an independent clause to attach it to. For instance, you might say, "Beyond a doubt, I will be at the wedding next Thursday."

4. Nobody.

This could be the subject or a different part of the sentence, called the object. For instance, the complete sentence might be, "Nobody in the room spoke up." It could also say, "I looked around, but I saw nobody."

5. While one wolf ate the meat.

This fragment almost seems like a complete sentence, except that the word *While* makes the reader wonder what else happened. The fragment is actually a dependent clause. This particular fragment could go at the beginning or the end of another clause to make a complete sentence. For example: "While one wolf ate the meat, the rest of the pack watched." or "The photographer took some pictures while one wolf ate the meat."

EXERCISE I:

Identify the following as "Fragment" or "Complete."

1. When I opened the door. **Fragment**

2. The box. **Fragment**

3. Considering the weather today, it's a miracle no one stayed home. **Complete**

4. This place is. **Fragment**

5. Because she saw Rico right before she left for the airport. **Fragment**

6. Whoever left the chair on the porch. **Fragment**

7. Kites flown in March. **Fragment**

8. Dreams of my childhood home still haunt me. **Complete**

9. Marcia and Dave, who work in the warehouse. **Fragment**

10. Have a meeting at four o'clock. **Fragment**

Teacher's Note: You can have students complete the fragments with words that turn the fragments into complete sentences. Further discussion could center on what grammatical part needs to be added to make each fragment a sentence.

In the following paragraphs, we have included numerous fragments. Although they seem to fit in the context of the paragraphs, these fragments cannot be left as they are. You need to eliminate all the fragments by rewriting them as complete sentences. For some, you may have to add words and for others, some words may need to be removed. There is not one perfect way to rewrite the paragraphs because the fragments can be corrected in a variety of ways. The only requirement is to eliminate every fragment.

Paragraph A

1) It was another freezing night out on the plains of the planet Xerxes. **2)** For the Captain of the Guards, Sir Kelling. **3)** He was constantly bothered by what he saw in the sky. **4)** Looking toward the north, he could just glimpse Earth. **5)** The planet he had left many years ago. **6)** He remembered what his life had been like. **7)** At only 25 years of age, Kelling had been dying. **8)** From the diseases. **9)** That were destroying most human life on Earth.

Answers will vary. Possible revision:

I) It was another freezing night out on the plains of the planet Xerxes for the Captain of the Guards, Sir Kelling. 2) He was constantly bothered by what he saw in the sky. 3) Looking toward the north, he could just glimpse Earth, the planet he had left many years ago. 4) He remembered what his life had been like. 5) At only 25 years of age, Kelling had been dying from the diseases that were destroying most human life on Earth.

Paragraph B

1) No one knew. **2)** Where these deadly germs had come from. **3)** Scientists, however, believed bacteria from a meteor that landed in Africa had carried one or two germs, which soon multiplied into a trillion killing machines. **4)** Sir Kelling had volunteered. **5)** To be part of an exploration. **6)** To search for other inhabitable worlds. **7)** Along with a crew of fifty other men and women from Earth, Kelling had blasted off into the unknown. **8)** Two hundred years before this night. **9)** The rocket had taken five years to arrive. **10)** On Xerxes by that time. **11)** Kelling was the only person left alive.

Answers will vary. Possible revision:

1) No one knew where these deadly germs had come from. 2) Scientists, however, believed bacteria from a meteor that landed in Africa had carried one or two germs, which soon multiplied into a trillion killing machines. 3) Sir Kelling had volunteered to be part of an exploration to search for other inhabitable worlds. 4) Along with a crew of fifty other men and women from Earth, Kelling had blasted off into the unknown two hundred years before this night. 5) The rocket had taken five years to arrive on Xerxes. 6) By that time, Kelling was the only person left alive.

Paragraph C

1) Lonely and alone. **2)** No one to talk to. **3)** And what was worse, no one to share the long, long rest of his life. **4)** Better off if he had simply died on the planet he now longed for. **5)** Who would want this horrible, almost never-ending type of existence? **6)** At least another thousand years. **7)** Before he would die peacefully. **8)** Everything necessary for life was easily available, though. **9)** Here on Xerxes. **10)** But the emptiness, the silence, and the lack of companionship. **11)** Were nearly driving him insane.

Answers will vary. Possible revision:

1) He was lonely and alone, with no one to talk to. 2) The worst part of life on Xerxes is that there was no one to share the long, long rest of his life. 3) It probably would have been better off if he had simply died on the planet he now longed for. 4) Who would want this horrible, almost never-ending type of existence of at least another thousand years? 5) Everything necessary for life was easily available, though, here on Xerxes. 6) The emptiness, the silence, and the lack of companionship were nearly driving him insane.

Chapter Four

Run-On Sentences

Earlier, you learned that in order for a sentence to be complete, it must have at least one independent clause and express a complete thought. Then, in the last chapter, you learned about fragments and their variations. Some sentences you will write, however, have more than one independent clause. Using more than one independent clause in a sentence *without linking them properly* is a serious mistake. This error is called a **run-on sentence**.

Look at the following sentence:

Wilma's purse was stolen Fred ran after the thief.
independent clause + independent clause = run-on

There are two entirely different thoughts in this run-on: 1) Someone stole Wilma's purse, and 2) Fred chased the thief. These two ideas cannot be in the same sentence as they are. They need to be joined or changed. Otherwise, the sentence is a run-on.

How could you make this a correct sentence and connect the thoughts? One of the easiest ways is to add a comma and a conjunction. Here are two examples:

Wilma's purse was stolen**, so** Fred ran after the thief.
independent clause + , conjunction + independent clause = sentence

Wilma's purse was stolen**, and** Fred ran after the thief.
independent clause + , conjunction + independent clause = sentence

You could also rewrite the sentence, as in these two examples:

Fred ran after the thief who had stolen Wilma's purse.

The second he saw that Wilma's purse had been stolen, Fred ran after the thief.

There are other ways to fix the problem of run-on sentences, and these are explained in more detail later in the chapter.

EXERCISE I:

The door was open, the cat got out, but did not go very far.

independent clause + independent clause = run-on

1. This run-on sentence contains three complete thoughts. What are they?

   1) The cat left. 2) The open door allowed the cat to escape. 3) The cat stayed close by.

2. Correct this run-on by using a comma and a conjunction and then by rewriting it using different words or a different arrangement.

   Answers will vary. Possible revisions:

   The door was open, and the cat got out, but did not go very far.

   Because the door was open, the cat got out, but she did not go very far.

   The cat did not go very far, even though she got out through the open door.

   The cat escaped through the open door, but she stayed nearby.

Now we are going to practice spotting run-on sentences and breaking them up into separate independent clauses.

Look at the following run-on sentences and draw a slanted line between the independent clauses. This will help you understand where the proper break between the thoughts and sentences should be. We have done one for you as an example:

Example:

My alarm didn't go off this morning I am furious because I will be late for school.
My alarm didn't go off this morning / I am furious because I will be late for school.

1. For breakfast, the elephants got more than 100 pounds of hay they ate it in a few minutes.

   For breakfast, the elephants got more than 100 pounds of hay / they ate it in a few minutes.

2. When you get to the intersection, turn left our house is on the left.

   When you get to the intersection, turn left / our house is on the left.

3. Make sure to buy Sal a notebook when you get to the store he needs one for school.

   Make sure to buy Sal a notebook when you get to the store / he needs one for school.

4. Have you seen that new movie it's hilarious.

   Have you seen that new movie / it's hilarious.

5. My computer's broken it crashed and the monitor turned black.

    My computer's broken / it crashed and the monitor turned black.

6. Gambling can be addictive, just like drugs after a while, it's difficult to stop.

    Gambling can be addictive, just like drugs / after a while, it's difficult to stop.

7. If Jon had seen the dollar, he would have picked it up because it was night, he didn't see it.

    If Jon had seen the dollar, he would have picked it up / because it was night, he didn't see it.

8. Snorkeling allowed her to see all the way to the bottom even though it was deep, Teri watched lobsters and starfish.

    Snorkeling allowed her to see all the way to the bottom / even though it was deep, Teri watched lobsters and starfish.

9. Next, the baker rolls the dough on a flat surface ten times this is to allow the bread to rise before it's put into the oven.

    Next, the baker rolls the dough on a flat surface ten times / this is to allow the bread to rise before it's put into the oven.

10. The death rate from lung cancer is falling therefore, scientists can conclude that fewer people are smoking cigarettes.

    The death rate from lung cancer is falling / therefore, scientists can conclude that fewer people are smoking cigarettes.

Teacher's Note: To extend this exercise, you might have students correct and rewrite the run-on sentences as a prelude to the more-thorough exercises in the next chapter. This could give classes a bit of a head start.

Draw a slanted line between the independent clauses that you find in the run-on sentences in the following paragraphs. There are quite a few run-on sentences, but there are also many that have no errors in them. You should leave these sentences alone.

Paragraph A

Emory hadn't finished his project he decided he would go to lunch later. There was a thunderstorm coming the sky was starting to get dark. He looked out the window and saw the first raindrops fall. Although he was glad not to be walking in the rain, Emory wished he were done with his work it seemed like this project was taking forever it felt impossible to concentrate. As he turned back to his computer, he suddenly had a great idea his fingers began typing a mile a minute.

Emory hadn't finished his project / he decided he would go to lunch later. There was a thunderstorm coming /the sky was starting to get dark. He looked out the window and saw the first raindrops fall. Although he was glad not to be walking in the rain, Emory wished he were done with his work / it seemed like this project was taking forever / it felt impossible to concentrate. As he turned back to his computer, he suddenly had a great idea / his fingers began typing a mile a minute.

Paragraph B

Kittens need to stay with their mothers until they are eight weeks old, at least. When a kitten is born, its eyes and ears are closed the mother cat has to take care of the kitten all the time. Since they are unable to regulate their own body temperature, kittens are kept warm by the mother if they lose too much heat they will die. Milk from the mother cat also protects the kitten against disease because of these issues, it is against the law to sell a kitten that is younger than eight weeks old.

Kittens need to stay with their mothers until they are eight weeks old, at least. When a kitten is born, its eyes and ears are closed / the mother cat has to take care of the kitten all the time. Since they are unable to regulate their own body temperature, kittens are kept warm by the mother / if they lose too much heat they will die. Milk from the mother cat also protects the kitten against disease / because of these issues, it is against the law to sell a kitten that is younger than eight weeks old.

Paragraph C

Selling goods or services to consumers depends on a product's brand the word *brand* means the name, the look, and the other things about a product this can include advertising, packaging design, ingredients, endorsements, etc. Sometimes a company will try something called "brand extension," which occurs when it starts a new line of products under its original brand. An example of this would be a soda company that starts making ice cream bars or a car company that also has a clothing line you see this all the time.

Selling goods or services to consumers depends on a product's brand / the word brand means the name, the look, and the other things about a product / this can include advertising, packaging design, ingredients, endorsements, etc. Sometimes a company will try something called "brand extension," which occurs when it starts a new line of products under its original brand. An example of this would be a soda company that starts making ice cream bars or a car company that also has a clothing line / you see this all the time.

Paragraph D

Although it would take only minutes to actually conduct the experiment, if the superconductor did not work, it would be months before the scientists could try again they were all crossing their fingers. The superconductor had taken ten years and billions of dollars to build. New ideas in nuclear physics might come out of the superconductor experiment on the other hand, everything could go horribly wrong. Many journalists were present at the powering up of the superconductor they wanted to see if it was worth all the hype.

Although it would take only minutes to actually conduct the experiment, if the superconductor did not work, it would be months before the scientists could try again / they were all crossing their fingers. The superconductor had taken ten years and billions of dollars to build. New ideas in nuclear physics might come out of the superconductor experiment / on the other hand, everything could go horribly wrong. Many journalists were present at the powering up of the superconductor / they wanted to see if it was worth all the hype.

Paragraph E

When Hurricane Katrina struck New Orleans, nearly everyone evacuated voluntarily there were some people, however, who did not leave. Many of them made the choice to stay others could not leave, though, because they didn't have transportation these people suffered the most. Katrina was the worst natural disaster ever in the United States it was even worse than the 1906 San Francisco Earthquake. Most of the dead in New Orleans died because their homes were flooded and there was no escape some people complained that the federal government did not do enough to help, but other people put the blame directly on the mayor of New Orleans. Reports show that levees that should have held back the water in the nearby lake failed these were designed improperly. Katrina will be a constant reminder of Nature's power and people's failures.

When Hurricane Katrina struck New Orleans, nearly everyone evacuated voluntarily / there were some people, however, who did not leave. Many of them made the choice to stay / others could not leave, though, because they didn't have transportation / these people suffered the most. Katrina was the worst natural disaster ever in the United States / it was even worse than the 1906 San Francisco Earthquake. Most of the dead in New Orleans died because their homes were flooded and there was no escape / some people complained that the federal government did not do enough to help, but other people put the blame directly on the mayor of New Orleans. Reports show that levees that should have held back the water in the nearby lake failed / these were designed improperly. Katrina will be a constant reminder of the power of Nature and the failings of people.

A Special Kind of Run-On: The Comma Splice

You have learned that a run-on sentence is made up of two independent clauses run together with nothing joining them. Sometimes people try to divide a run-on sentence with only a comma. A comma is not strong enough, however, to divide two independent clauses. When a comma is used by itself to join independent clauses, it is called a **comma splice**.

One of the easiest ways to correct a comma splice, however, is simply by adding a good conjunction after the comma. Look back on page 18 at the examples about Wilma's purse, and you will see some ways this error can be fixed.

> **Remember**: *A comma, by itself, is not strong enough to split up two*
> **(!)**   *independent clauses.*

Here are some examples of comma splices:

Darryl read five books last month, his favorite was by Stephen King.
independent clause, + independent clause = comma splice

This incorrect sentence is made up of two independent clauses—"Darryl read five books last month"—and—"his favorite was by Stephen King." There is no connection between the two, however. The sentence needs a conjunction to join the different thoughts. Otherwise, it is a comma splice. This comma splice can be fixed by adding the conjunction *but*.

Darryl read five books last month, **but** his favorite was by Stephen King.
independent clause, + conjunction + independent clause = sentence

Bring the tickets to the concert, don't be late.
independent clause, + independent clause = comma splice

One conjunction that works to correct this comma splice is *and*. The word *but* is another conjunction that could fit into the sentence. It all depends on the idea the writer wants to convey.

Bring the tickets to the concert, **and** don't be late.
independent clause, + conjunction + independent clause = sentence

Correct the comma splice in each of the following sentences by adding a conjunction that fits the meaning of the sentence. You may think that the comma splice would be better if you corrected the error by writing two separate sentences, but for this exercise, concentrate on using good conjunctions.

1. Dad made us pancakes, he forgot to make scrambled eggs.

   Dad made us pancakes, but he forgot to make scrambled eggs.

2. While you were running for Student Council, you made enemies as well as friends, now it's time to reconcile with those you offended.

   While you were running for Student Council, you made enemies as well as friends, so now it's time to reconcile with those you offended.

3. Swimming to the side of the pool, Larry caught his breath, he wasn't sure what had just happened.

   Swimming to the side of the pool, Larry caught his breath, but he wasn't sure what had just happened.

4. Maybe the monster will come back, this time, we will be ready.

   Maybe the monster will come back, and this time, we will be ready.

5. As Tamiko was walking down Chestnut Street, she passed a shop with beautiful flowers in the window, she decided to go inside.

   As Tamiko was walking down Chestnut Street, she passed a shop with beautiful flowers in the window, so she decided to go inside.

6. I'll have two orders of cheese fries, I want the second one without onions.

   I'll have two orders of cheese fries, but I want the second one without onions.

7. We all thought Pete would be the winner of the race, he didn't do his best.

   We all thought Pete would be the winner of the race, but he didn't do his best.

8. Finish blowing up the balloons, I'll put the icing on the cake.

   Finish blowing up the balloons, and I'll put the icing on the cake.

9. April is National Poetry Month, let's write a poem.

   April is National Poetry Month, so let's write a poem.

10. Angel wants to add a room to his house soon, we can't paint it until winter.

    Angel wants to add a room to his house soon, but we can't paint it until winter.

There are other ways of fixing run-on sentences and comma splices, though. If there were not, your writing would soon be very boring. You have learned two already—using a comma and conjunction, or rewriting the sentence using different words. Another method of correcting run-ons and comma splices is to break them into separate sentences by using a period and a capital letter. Look at the following examples:

My new computer game is in the mail, my mom ordered it just two days ago.
independent clause, + independent clause = comma splice

The members of the Supreme Court met today they decided to hear a case on spying.
independent clause + independent clause = run-on

You certainly could fix the problems by using a comma and conjunction, but you can also make each example into two sentences.

My new computer game is in the mail. My mom ordered it just two days ago.
sentence   **sentence**

The members of the Supreme Court met today. They decided to hear a case on spying.
sentence   **sentence**

Of course, if all your sentences are like these two corrected ones, your writing will soon become repetitious. Therefore, there are other methods that can fix comma splices and run-ons. Instead of adding a comma and conjunction, rewriting, or using a period, you can break up sentences with these errors in them by using a semicolon. Take a look at these examples that need to be corrected:

Darlene visited her grandfather last week, it was his 90th birthday.
independent clause, + independent clause = comma splice

I need to know who spilled the milk, tell me immediately!
independent clause, + independent clause = comma splice

Don't use that weird font I think it's really ugly.
independent clause + independent clause = run-on

The natives were able to make everything from plants watching them work was amazing.
independent clause + independent clause = run-on

Now, look at them when a semicolon has been inserted to correct them:

Darlene visited her grandfather last week; it was his 90th birthday.
independent clause + ; independent clause = sentence

I need to know who spilled the milk; tell me immediately!
independent clause + ; independent clause = sentence

Don't use that weird font; I think it's really ugly.
independent clause + ; independent clause = sentence

The natives were able to make everything from plants; watching them work was amazing.
independent clause + ; independent clause = sentence

You should not use a semicolon, however, when the independent clauses are not closely related. In the following run-on sentence, the ideas are not closely related, so a different correction method should be used:

I like spearmint bubblegum baseball is an exciting sport.
independent clause + independent clause = run-on

This sentence should be rewritten because the ideas are so disconnected.

Spearmint is my favorite gum. I love chewing it during exciting baseball games.
sentence   **sentence**

You will frequently like the sentence the way you wrote it and will not want to reword it; therefore, you will need other ways to break up a run-on or comma splice so that your reader understands where each thought starts and stops. Luckily, English has five methods that let you do this. You have covered four already:

- using a comma and conjunction
- rewriting
- using a period
- using a semicolon

Remember that these methods are not interchangeable. Sometimes, you'll want to use a particular one, but other sentences will need something different. It depends on how the independent clauses relate to each other, and it depends on how you want to express your thoughts.

The final way to correct a few kinds of run-ons and comma splices is to use a colon. A colon shows that there is going to be further information or explanation. When you see a sentence with a colon in it, you could think, "What's next?" The words that come after the colon explain or expand upon the idea that comes before it. Look at what is explained in this example:

Dustin knew one thing his home run had won the game.
independent clause + independent clause = run-on

You can see that this run-on sentence is made up of two different ideas: 1) Dustin understood something, and 2) His home run was the winning hit. Both these ideas cannot exist in the same sentence as it is.

A comma and conjunction does not fit: The sentence would read something like, "Dustin knew one thing, and his home run had won the game." This makes no logical sense.

Making it into two sentences gives you this: "Dustin knew one thing. His home run had won the game." The two sentences are very closely related, though, so separating them is not the answer.

Adding a semicolon, a third way to fix the run-on, is basically the same as using a period: It does not keep the ideas together.

The fourth method, rewriting, is a possibility: "Dustin realized that his home run had won the game." This way does work, but there is a better solution.

This run-on sentence really would benefit from a colon, which is a mark of punctuation that alerts the reader that more information will be explained in the rest of the sentence. For example:

Dustin knew one thing: his home run had won the game.
independent clause + : independent clause = sentence

The colon tells the reader, "This is the one thing Dustin knew." When you see the colon, you wonder what he knew, and the independent clause that comes after the colon specifically explains what Dustin's belief was.

Of all five methods, the colon is the one that writers use least frequently, but it is a valuable tool to use in your writing.

Decide whether each of the following sentences contains a fragment, is a run-on, a comma splice, or is correct. Place the letters **F** (fragment), **R** (run-on), **S** (comma splice), or **C** (correct) in the blanks. If a sentence is incorrect, fix it by what you think is the best method for that sentence. You can either use proper punctuation or rewrite it.

Teacher's Note: As these are the most common errors in student writing, we have made this exercise longer than the others. Because there are many variations for potential rewrites, we have supplied only a few. Accept answers that make sense and are correct.

To extend this exercise, have students who need extra help, or the entire class, read the sentences aloud before completing the exercise. Hearing how they would naturally speak the sentences will probably help those who do not quite understand the concept.

F 1. Chef Stephano will put pickles on your hamburger. Unless you specifically ask him not to.

Chef Stephano will put pickles on your hamburger, unless you specifically ask him not to.

OR

Unless you specifically ask him not to, Chef Stephano will put pickles on your hamburger.

R 2. Cindy likes peppermint ice cream her brother Brad prefers chocolate.

Cindy likes peppermint ice cream, but her brother Brad prefers chocolate.

OR

Cindy likes peppermint ice cream. Her brother Brad prefers chocolate.

R 3. The twins couldn't make it to the wedding they had to take care of their sick father.

The twins couldn't make it to the wedding; they had to take care of their sick father.

OR

The twins couldn't make it to the wedding because they had to take care of their sick father.

F 4. Although the work is hard at first; it does get easier if you just keep doing it.

Although the work is hard at first, it does get easier if you just keep doing it.

R 5. Sam didn't bring his umbrella he knew Brandon would have one.

Sam didn't bring his umbrella; he knew Brandon would have one.

OR

Sam didn't bring his umbrella because he knew Brandon would have one.

OR

Sam didn't bring his umbrella, but he knew Brandon would have one.

OR

Sam didn't bring his umbrella. He knew Brandon would have one.

F 6. Lunch with her favorite tennis player was so amazing; that Yvette never wanted it to end.

Lunch with her favorite tennis player was so amazing that Yvette never wanted it to end.

S 7. Al decided to buy a lottery ticket, he needed some good luck.

Al decided to buy a lottery ticket; he needed some good luck.

__R__ 8. Once the reporter had finished the interview, she put her notes away I noticed that she put them in the side pocket of her bag.

Once the reporter had finished the interview, she put her notes away. I noticed that she put them in the side pocket of her bag.

__S__ 9. Only one theory exists to explain the robbery, someone from the bank is involved.

Only one theory exists to explain the robbery: Someone from the bank is involved.

__C__ 10. None of the students knew the answer to the math problem, but the teacher was able to explain it.

__C__ 11. Several bright orange goldfish swam in the pond, and sunlight fell through the water.

__R__ 12. Connie will not be going to the movie tonight she sure wants to, though.

Connie will not be going to the movie tonight; she sure wants to, though.

　　OR

Connie will not be going to the movie tonight. She sure wants to, though.

　　OR

Connie will not be going to the movie tonight, but she sure wants to.

__S__ 13. When you see the barn on your left, turn right, if you go past a dentist's office, you've gone too far.

When you see the barn on your left, turn right; if you go past a dentist's office, you've gone too far.

_S_ 14. Considering how much money has been spent on the bridge so far, it should be the most advanced structure in the world, I can't wait to see it.

Considering how much money has been spent on the bridge so far, it should be the most advanced structure in the world; I can't wait to see it.

_C_ 15. James carefully read what I had typed out, and then he paused and gathered his thoughts.

_R_ 16. Mrs. Delancey's window broke yesterday during the storm it hadn't been installed properly in the first place.

Mrs. Delancey's window broke yesterday during the storm, but it hadn't been installed properly in the first place.

_R_ 17. Tony loves going to Michael's house for dinner he turned down Michael's invitation today.

Tony loves going to Michael's house for dinner, but he turned down Michael's invitation today.

_R_ 18. Write a story about a spaceship use your imagination.

Write a story about a spaceship. Use your imagination.

_S_ 19. I have something hilarious to tell you, Sara wants to date my brother.

I have something hilarious to tell you: Sara wants to date my brother.

_C_ 20. Although Bella can hear people talking, it's hard for her to understand their words.

_F_ 21. If it's not hard to put a bookshelf together. Why is it taking this long?

If it's not hard to put a bookshelf together, why is it taking this long?

_S_ 22. Elijah can take advanced math, he can take introductory German instead.

Elijah can take advanced math, or he can take introductory German instead.

__C__ 23. Because I knew I couldn't finish the book before Wednesday, I tried to renew it at the library, but someone else had already requested it.

__R__ 24. When Nasir needed money for the fair, he decided to ask around the neighborhood he discovered that many people had been looking for babysitters.

When Nasir needed money for the fair, he decided to ask around the neighborhood, and he discovered that many people had been looking for babysitters.

> **OR**

When Nasir needed money for the fair, he decided to ask around the neighborhood; he discovered that many people had been looking for babysitters.

__R__ 25. Parents teach their children many important skills how to ride a bicycle, how to cross a street safely, how to tie a shoe, and how to tell time.

Parents teach their children many important skills: how to ride a bicycle, how to cross a street safely, how to tie a shoe, and how to tell time.

__S__ 26. You are my best friend, Kathy Marie is second.

You are my best friend, Kathy. Marie is second. [First girl is named Kathy.]

> **OR**

You are my best friend; Kathy Marie is second. [First girl is unnamed; second is Kathy Marie.]

__S__ 27. You need to explain the answer, I do not understand it.

You need to explain the answer because I do not understand it.

> **OR**

You need to explain the answer; I do not understand it.

__C__ 28. My computer just crashed, and I don't know when I can finish the job, so I need an extension.

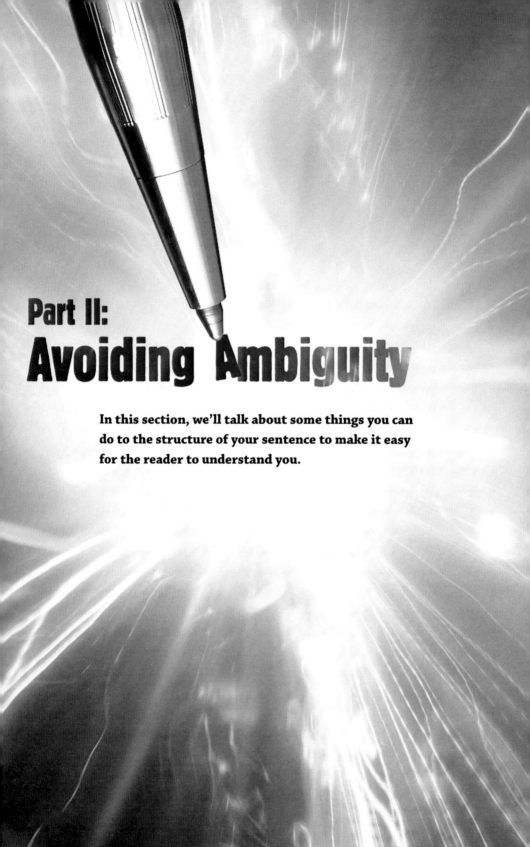

Part II:
Avoiding Ambiguity

In this section, we'll talk about some things you can do to the structure of your sentence to make it easy for the reader to understand you.

Chapter One

Modifiers

A **modifier** is a word or phrase that gives additional information about a certain part of the sentence. If a modifier is in the wrong place, it may confuse your reader. These errors are easy to spot when they obviously make the sentence mean something other than what it *should* mean. The word *only* is a simple modifier, yet it can change the meaning of a sentence dramatically. Look at this comment:

I *only* punched Thomas in his arm.

The sentence means that the one thing that I did was to punch Thomas in his arm. However, if the word *only* is moved to different places in the sentence, the meaning is very different:

- *Only* I punched Thomas in his arm. (No one else punched Thomas.)
- I punched *only* Thomas in his arm. (I did not punch anyone else.)
- I punched Thomas *only* in his arm. (I did not punch Thomas anywhere else.)
- I punched Thomas in his *only* arm. (Thomas had just one arm.)

It should be clear just from this one example that placement of words, or phrases, is essential to understanding the meaning the writer intended. With a word like *only*, it is easy to see the confusion that the misplaced modifier can cause, but with other, less obvious errors, it can be more difficult, and you need to be more careful.

In all of the following examples, the modifiers are *italicized*, and the words they modify are <u>underlined</u>. The rule is that the modifier should go next to, or very close to, the noun it modifies. For instance, look at Sentence A:

A) *Clapping his hands*, <u>the dancer</u> moved in a circle.
      modifier   **noun**

The modifier, "Clapping his hands," explains what "the dancer" did. In Sentence B, however, the modifier is in the wrong place.

B) *Listening for sounds,* <u>the killer's shoes</u> made noises.
    modifier   **noun**

This sentence makes it sound like the killer's shoes have ears that can hear sounds. Of course, this is wrong. One way to correct this problem is to rewrite the sentence, adding the correct noun that *Listening for sounds* modifies. What or who would be listening for the killer's shoes?

Listening for sounds, <u>the detectives</u> heard the killer's shoes make noises.
    modifier   **noun**

Sometimes, with misplaced modifiers, the subject of the modifier doesn't even appear in the sentence, as in Sentence C:

C) *Laughing and talking,* <u>the night</u> flew by.
    modifier   **noun**

Who was laughing and talking? It probably wasn't the night; some people must have been involved. The subject of the modifying phrase, *Laughing and talking,* cannot be "the night." Something else has to be laughing and talking, but nothing in the sentence can perform those actions.

Here are some ways you might correct the sentence by adding in the people doing the action of laughing and talking:

Laughing and talking, <u>we</u> saw the night fly by.
    modifier   **pronoun**

While <u>they</u> were *laughing and talking,* the night flew by.
    pronoun   **modifier**

Many times, misplaced modifiers make sentences seem ridiculous. What is the real meaning that the writer is trying to convey in Sentence D?

D) Chrissy wore a <u>green ribbon</u> in her hair, *which had an odd shape.*
               noun   **modifier**

You know that the ribbon is green and is in a weird shape, but the sentence really does mean that Chrissy's hair had an odd shape. The modifying part of the sentence, *which had an odd shape*, is in the wrong place. Here are some ways you might correct the sentence:

Chrissy wore a <u>green ribbon</u>, *which had an odd shape*, in her hair.
               noun   **modifier**

Chrissy wore an *oddly shaped* <u>green ribbon</u> in her hair.
              modifier   **noun**

Misplaced modifiers can also be present if you use them carelessly, as in Sentence E:

E) I eat my usual dinner at that new <u>restaurant</u>, *which is composed of steak, potatoes, and dessert.*
                                    noun   **modifier**

Doesn't that sentence mean that the restaurant is made of steak, potatoes, and dessert? Yes, it does. Here is one way you might correct this sentence:

I eat my usual <u>dinner</u>, *steak, potatoes, and dessert*, at that new restaurant.
              noun   **modifier**

You saw that starting sentences with *ing* words can cause modifier problems as in examples A, B, and C. Another, similar sentence construction can also make your sentences awkward if you do not use it carefully. Using verbs with *ed* on the end to begin sentences can lead to confusion and errors. Here is an example:

F) *Placed in the refrigerator*, my friend <u>Sally</u> wanted the apple pie.
      modifier   **noun**

The sentence is supposed to mean that Sally is hungry for an apple pie that was put in her refrigerator. Because of the incorrect placement, however, it really means that Sally was put into the refrigerator.

Here is one change that could correct the sentence. All it took was rewording the sentence and using the modifier correctly by placing it closer to the word it affects.

After she placed the apple pie in the refrigerator, my friend <u>Sally</u> wanted it.
    modifier   **noun**

Many times, prepositional phrases can cause confusion if they are misplaced. Prepositional phrases should also be placed close to the word they modify. Look at Sentence G to see an example of this type of error.

G) Grandmother was wondering what she would <u>do</u> *on her Christmas vacation.*
              verb **modifier**

In this sentence, was it on her Christmas vacation that Grandmother was wondering what she would do? Or was she wondering about doing something *when the time came* for her Christmas vacation? It is impossible to tell, simply because of the misplaced prepositional phrase. Your sentences need to be specific, so anyone who reads what you write will understand what you want to say. With unclear prepositional phrases like this one, simply moving the prepositional phrase may solve the problem—you may need to rewrite part of the sentence so it is correct. Here are two examples:

On her Christmas vacation, <u>Grandmother</u> was wondering what she would do.
 modifier   **noun**

Grandmother was wondering what she would <u>do</u> *for her Christmas vacation.*
             verb **modifier**

Rewrite the sentences so that they are correct by fixing the misplaced modifiers. The first one has been done for you as an example.

Teacher's Note: We have supplied potential alternative answers; students will certainly come up with others. Any sentences that solve the modifier issues should be accepted.

1. Opening the can of cat food, the cats cried at my feet.

    Opening the can of cat food, I saw the cats crying at my feet.

    OR

    Seeing me open the can of cat food, the cats cried at my feet.

2. Evan reported that the horse was winning the race, appearing surprised.

    Evan, appearing surprised, reported that the horse was winning the race.

    OR

    Evan seemed surprised when he reported that the horse was winning the race.

3. The constellation seemed much brighter looking through the telescope.

    Viewed through the telescope, the constellation seemed much brighter.

    OR

    When I viewed it through the telescope, the constellation seemed much brighter.

4. Cupping his hand to his ear, a roar went up for Mr. Carrot, the team's mascot.

   Cupping his hand to his ear, Mr. Carrot, the team's mascot, drew a roar from the crowd.

   ### OR

   Mr. Carrot, the team's mascot, drew a roar from the crowd when he cupped his hand to his ear.

5. Taking a big bite of the donut, the jelly squirted all over Enrique's nose.

   Taking a big bite of the donut, Enrique squirted jelly all over his nose.

   ### OR

   Enrique squirted jelly all over his nose when he took a big bite of the donut.

6. Many pioneers were amazed at the sun's power, moving swiftly across the sky.

   Many pioneers were amazed at the sun's power as it moved swiftly across the sky.

   ### OR

   The power of the sun, as it moved across the sky, was amazing to the pioneers.

7. We had heard that Frank wanted to be cremated before his death.

   Before his death, we had heard that Frank wanted to be cremated.

8.   I saw a Ford that could go 200 mph in my neighbor's garage.

In my neighbor's garage, I saw a Ford that could go 200 mph.

Explain, if necessary, that the following revision is also incorrect:

I saw a Ford in my neighbor's garage that could go 200 mph.

9.   The home in the valley built mainly of oak and maple was destroyed by the fire.

The home, built mainly of oak and maple, was destroyed by the fire.

OR

In the valley, the fire destroyed the home that was built mainly of oak and maple.

OR

The oak and maple home in the valley was destroyed by the fire.

10.   The scientist said that tigers are not dangerous to people on television.

The scientist on television said that tigers are not dangerous to people.

OR

While on television, the scientist said that tigers are not dangerous to people.

11. Ralph saw many different plants and animals traveling around the country.

    Traveling around the country, Ralph saw many different plants and animals.

    OR

    While he was traveling around the country, Ralph saw many different plants and animals.

12. Some of our country's energy needs could be met by a natural-gas pipeline going into the future.

    In the future, some of our country's energy needs could be met by a natural-gas pipeline.

    OR

    As we go into the future, some of our country's energy needs could be met by a natural-gas pipeline.

13. Unfortunately, we left the meeting with the new employee under the wrong impression.

    Unfortunately, when we left the meeting with the new employee, we were under the wrong impression.

    OR

    Unfortunately, the new employee was under the wrong impression when we left the meeting.

14. Mom may find the house of her dreams taking a tour around the neighborhood.

    Taking a tour of the neighborhood, Mom may find the house of her dreams.

    OR

    While she is touring the neighborhood, Mom may find the house of her dreams.

15. Danielle saw a big squirrel riding her bicycle this morning.

    Riding her bicycle this morning, Danielle saw a big squirrel.

    OR

    Danielle saw a big squirrel while she was riding her bicycle this morning.

16. I saw Mrs. Arnold's dog barking loudly at the front door.

    When I stood at the front door, I saw Mrs. Arnold's dog barking loudly.

    OR

    I saw Mrs. Arnold's dog barking loudly and scratching at the front door.

17. Sam found the quilt that Moni had given him behind the house.

    Behind the house, Sam found the quilt that Moni had given him.

    OR

    Sam found the quilt, which Moni had given him, behind the house. (Sam found the quilt behind the house.)

    OR

    Sam found the quilt, which Moni had given him behind the house. (Moni gave Sam the quilt behind the house.)

18. Laila received a big round of applause from her friends going up to the stage.

Going up to the stage, Laila received a big round of applause from her friends.

OR

Laila's friends gave her a big round of applause as she went up to the stage.

19. Reading *The New York Times*, the second story surprised us.

We were reading *The New York Times*, and the second story surprised us.

OR

Having read *The New York Times*, we were surprised by the second story.

20. To be a successful politician, understanding people's needs is essential.

For a person to be a successful politician, he or she must understand people's needs.

OR

Understanding people's needs is essential if someone wants to be a successful politician.

Teacher's Note: We have not made a formal distinction between "misplaced" and "dangling" modifiers since the exact nature of the difference may not be necessary for students who need some remedial assistance in avoiding them.

Chapter Two

Tenses

The **tense** of a verb shows when it happened. Look at these sentences, which are all the same, *except* for the verb tense:

1. Jerry walks by my desk every morning.
2. Jerry walked by my desk every morning.
3. Jerry will walk by my desk every morning.

Just by understanding the tense, we know that Sentence 1 means that Jerry does this activity every day. Sentence 2 means that he used to do it. Sentence 3 means that he may or may not have done it previously, but he will in the future. The basic rule of tenses is to keep all verbs in their proper time and not to shift the tense, unless it is necessary.

4. Gerard kicks the table, and papers flew everywhere.
5. The summer of 2006 was hot, so there is a poor wheat harvest.

In this part of Sentence 4, *Gerard kicks the table*, you can assume that Gerald is kicking the table *now*. This is a present tense verb. However, if that is true, how can the *papers flew everywhere*? The word *flew* is in the past tense; this means that the papers were scattered *before* the table was kicked, which is impossible.

In Sentence 5, the tenses are reversed: The heat of summer in 2006 caused a bad harvest in the present. This sequence of verb tense makes no sense.

Try to fix sentences 4 and 5 so they use the correct tense.

Teacher's Note: Most answers for these two will be correct, but make sure to ask any students who have shifts in their verbs or who have an incorrect verb order to explain their choice of tense.

Gerard kicked the table, and papers flew everywhere.

OR

Gerard kicks the table, and papers fly everywhere.

The summer of 2006 was hot, so there was a poor wheat harvest.

Be careful not to switch tenses in the middle of your sentence. If you do this, your reader won't know when the action took place. For example, read Paragraph A. We have italicized the verbs so you can recognize them easily:

Paragraph A

Charles Morse and the Heinze brothers, Augustus and Otto, *corner* the market on copper, which *leads* to the Panic of 1907. Augustus Heinze *was owning* the United Copper Company, *forced* people who *buy* the stock to pay a higher price for it. The brothers *are going* to buy up shares of United Copper so they *controlled* the price. People who *own* stock in United Copper *are* not able to pay the price that the Heinze brothers *will want*, causing the bank to fail. The entire economy *might collapse* because there *is* a run on the banks. J.P. Morgan *heads* a group of bankers who *pledged* their own money to keep the stock exchange and the banks intact. This promise *causes* the U.S. economy not to fail.

From this paragraph, we might get a general sense of some of the things that happened, but it's hard to say what came first, when things happened, what was the cause and what was the effect. Compare Paragraph A to Paragraph B. This paragraph is exactly the same as A, except for the needed tense changes.

Paragraph B

Charles Morse and the Heinze brothers, Augustus and Otto, *cornered* the market on copper, which *led* to the Panic of 1907. Augustus Heinze *owned* the United Copper Company, *forcing* people who *bought* the stock to pay a higher price for it. The brothers *were going* to buy up shares of United Copper so they *could control* the price. People who *owned* stock in United Copper *were* not able to pay the price that the Heinze brothers *wanted*, causing the bank to fail. The entire economy *might have collapsed* because there was a run on the banks. J.P. Morgan *headed* a group of bankers who *pledged* their own money to keep the stock exchange and the banks intact. This promise *caused* the U.S. economy not to fail.

Paragraph B is a great deal easier to understand, simply because of keeping the verb tenses in the past. Since it is about something that happened in 1907, using past tense makes the most sense.

EXERCISE II:

Correct the tense problems in the following sentences. Most can be corrected in more than one way, but all sentences contain errors.

Answers will vary.

1. The bank will not approve the loan because it was too risky.

    The bank would not approve the loan because it was too risky.

2. Does Abe Lincoln really believed the words in the quote?

    Did Abe Lincoln really believe the words in the quote?

3. If we have been allowed to attend the show, everything would have been different.

    If we had been allowed to attend the show, everything would have been different.

4. The game that the team plays the month before was on the quarterback's mind.

   The game that the team played the month before was on the quarterback's mind.

5. In 2036, it will have been one hundred years since the bill has been passed.

   In 2036, it will be one hundred years since the bill was passed.

6. Until we discover the memo, we thought we will have to recreate the files.

   Until we discovered the memo, we thought we would have to recreate the files.

7. Lizzie had not gotten as much work done as she thinks she would.

   Lizzie has not gotten as much work done as she thought she should have.

8. Because the washing machine is broken this morning, Deirdre could not wash the dishes.

   Because the washing machine broke this morning, Deirdre could not wash the dishes.

9. Having been a preschool teacher for ten years, Greg learns a few things about raising kids.

   Having been a preschool teacher for ten years, Greg learned a few things about raising kids.

10. The detective was sure that Veronica is telling the truth, but he still believes the explosion is not an accident.

    The detective was sure that Veronica was telling the truth, but he still believed the explosion was not an accident.

11. Whenever you do a crossword puzzle, you were stimulating cells in your brain.

    Whenever you do a crossword puzzle, you are stimulating cells in your brain.

12. When he was twelve, Bert has moved from Chicago to New York.

    When he was twelve, Bert moved from Chicago to New York.

13. I know you got your start in a small local theatre, but you soon become famous.

    I know you got your start in a small local theatre, but you will soon become famous.

14. Yesterday, in the office, Charles becomes ill and goes home.

    Yesterday, in the office, Charles became ill and went home.

15. My dictionary was the best because it has some definitions that the others didn't.

    My dictionary is the best because it has some definitions that the others don't.

Rewrite this paragraph, making sure that all tenses are correct. To make it a little more challenging, we have not identified the verbs.

In the past year, in one big-city suburb, members of a gang will award points to other teenagers, who are not yet in gangs, for vandalizing portions of their enemies' neighborhoods. In 2007, a 16-year-old in California takes some classmates to look at the body he finds. None of them tell police about it. Later, the boy will be charged with murder. In Miami, Florida, more than 40 teenagers are arrested for murder in the past two years. This trend of lawlessness among teenagers represented a frightening situation in America. What will be behind this alarming growth of anti-social behavior? Was it television? Was it related to the breakup of the traditional family? Were these issues part of the influence movies and music had on teenagers? No scientists were able to provide an answer. We must have asked these young people themselves.

In the past year, in one big-city suburb, members of a gang awarded points to other teenagers, who were not yet in gangs, for vandalizing portions of their enemies' neighborhoods. In 2007, a 16-year-old in California took some classmates to look at the body he had found. None of them told police about it. Later, the boy was charged with murder. In Miami, Florida, more than 40 teenagers have been arrested for murder in the past two years. This trend of lawlessness among teenagers represents a frightening situation in America. What is behind this alarming growth of anti-social behavior? Is it television? Is it related to the breakup of the traditional family? Are these issues part of the influence movies and music have on teenagers? No scientists are able to provide an answer. We must ask these young people themselves.

Chapter Three

Series

A list of three or more items in a sentence is called a **series**. A series can be made up of nouns, adjectives, verbs, or even independent clauses. Each of the following sentences contains a series. The series in each sentence is underlined:

- In English class, we are learning about <u>nouns, verbs, adjectives, and adverbs</u>.
- <u>Painting, sculpting, and drawing</u> are taught by Mrs. Han.
- For lunch, you can have <u>meat, fish, or salad</u>.
- The whale <u>surfaced, blew out a stream of water, and dove down again</u>.
- President Roosevelt was elected in <u>1932, 1936, 1940, and 1944</u>.
- <u>Playing sports, reading magazines, and taking pictures</u> used to be my favorite hobbies.
- The star of the movie <u>packed his clothing, called a taxi, and then left the movie set</u>.

It's important to use a comma after each item in the series *except the last* so that your reader knows which words go together. For instance, look at the following sentence:

The breakfast cafe serves <u>Oaties, Wheat Flakes, and Strawberry Dunkers</u>.

Without the commas, it looks like this:

The breakfast cafe serves Oaties Wheat Flakes and Strawberry Dunkers.

Without the commas, a reader might get the impression that the breakfast cafe serves only two items: 1) Oaties Wheat Flakes and 2) Strawberry Dunkers. The café, however, really sells three items: 1) Oaties, 2) Wheat Flakes, and 3) Strawberry Dunkers. When the series is properly punctuated, there are only two commas in it. In addition, the series is not separated from the rest of the sentence with a comma.

Here is another example:

> Bette and Alyson watched the school drill team rehearse, played some music and video games, went for a ride, and visited my cousin at the beach last weekend.

How many things did the girls do? Four. They *watched*, *played*, *went*, and *visited*. One important rule is that a comma always needs to separate the second-to-last item in the series from the conjunction. (In a series, the words *and* or *or* are usually the conjunctions.)

You might also wonder why there is no comma after *music*. The series represents a list of things Bette and Alyson did. 'Music and video games,' though, are the objects of *played*. Ask yourself what did Bette and Alyson *play*? The answer is that they played two things—music and video games. Listing two items does not make a grammatical series; therefore, it does not need a comma.

In the next sentence, notice that Harry accomplished five things. You will see that there are only four commas in the series. They are shown in bold.

> Harry had <u>fixed the roof</u>**,** <u>dug out the dead tree stump</u>**,** <u>mended the fence</u>**,** <u>repaired the well</u>**,** and <u>balanced the front door</u>.

From this example, we can establish a rule for commas in a series: There will always be one fewer comma than there are items in a series. This means that if Harry had done 108 things, you would need 107 commas.

The only exception to the rule is when there are only two items in the series, as we stated previously. No comma is used with two items because the conjunction takes the place of the comma, as in this example:

> Harry had <u>fixed the roof</u> and <u>dug out the dead tree stump</u>.

Use the rules you have learned about commas in series to punctuate the following sentences. One sentence is correct as written.

1. Lettuce carrots and peas grew in the garden this summer.

    Lettuce, carrots, and peas grew in the garden this summer.

2. We read one of Miranda Carlyle's books in class and wrote letters to her.

    Correct

3. The parts of the party that thrilled my little brother the most were the cake the games the presents and the pony rides.

    The parts of the party that thrilled my little brother the most were the cake, the games, the presents, and the pony rides.

4. My kitten ate her food chased a toy around the room played with her mother and fell asleep immediately afterwards.

    My kitten ate her food, chased a toy around the room, played with her mother, and fell asleep immediately afterwards.

5. For the picnic, the wrestling team purchased three loaves of bread for their sandwiches five pounds of meat two jars each of mustard and relish twenty-four sodas three bags of potato chips and not one fresh vegetable.

    For the picnic, the wrestling team purchased three loaves of bread for their sandwiches, five pounds of meat, two jars each of mustard and relish, twenty-four sodas, three bags of potato chips, and not one fresh vegetable.

6. Do you like hiking biking or skateboarding?

    Do you like hiking, biking, or skateboarding?

7. The rain was continuing to fall the reservoir was starting to overflow and the town's two dams were showing signs of cracking.

   The rain was continuing to fall, the reservoir was starting to overflow, and the town's two dams were showing signs of cracking.

8. Jim won't be at the meeting the presentation ceremony or the party after work.

   Jim won't be at the meeting, the presentation ceremony, or the party after work.

9. The store sold paper pens and pencils envelopes stamps and dictionaries.

   The store sold paper, pens and pencils, envelopes, stamps, and dictionaries.

10. Did you ever have potato chips bananas and peanut butter and jelly on a sandwich?

    Did you ever have potato chips, bananas, and peanut butter and jelly on a sandwich?

Semicolon Use in Series

If the items in a series are simple and have no other punctuation in them, you should use a comma to separate them. For example, in the following sentence, commas are good enough:

There are ducks, geese, and chickens wandering around the farm.

What would happen, though, if the writer wanted to give you more facts about the three types of animals on the farm? For instance, look at some additional information that the writer now wants to include in the sentence:

- The ducks are sold to nearby restaurants to help pay expenses.
- The geese used to be wild, but now they are tame and, therefore, are not sold.
- The chickens are used primarily for their eggs, not as food.

It would be nearly impossible to include all of it in one sentence using only commas and have the reader understand it easily. Look at how complicated it would appear:

> There are ducks, which are sold to nearby restaurants to help pay expenses, geese, which used to be wild, but are now tame and, therefore, do not get sold, and chickens that are used primarily for their eggs, not as food, wandering around the farm.

The series must be broken up with **semicolons**. Semicolons make it much easier to read and understand:

> There are ducks, which are sold to nearby restaurants to help pay expenses; geese, which used to be wild, but are now tame and, therefore, do not get sold; and chickens that are used primarily for their eggs, not as food, wandering around the farm.

You will often have a series in which some items contain two or more parts and require additional punctuation. In this case, you must use a semicolon, not a comma, to break up the series. For instance, look at this sentence:

> The park has a swing and a huge, red slide, which is plastic and is about four feet by twenty feet long nature paths, which I've found suitable for hiking and biking, although they are a bit too muddy in the spring and picnic areas, which can be reserved by calling the Parks Service.

It's hard to tell what goes with what in this sentence. Are the nature paths *long*, or is *long* part of the size of the slide? Are the paths muddy around the picnic areas or just in the spring? That's why we need to break up the series with semicolons.

> The park has a swing and a huge, red slide, which is plastic and is about four feet by twenty feet long; nature paths, which I've found suitable for hiking and biking, although they are a bit too muddy in the spring; and picnic areas, which can be reserved by calling the Parks Service.

Here's another example of a long series in which only commas are used. Note how confusing it is:

> On my desk, I always have a brand-new dictionary, which was invaluable when I was learning English—I buy a new one each year to see words that have recently come into English usage—at least one encyclopedia, a thesaurus, which helps me use more interesting words, pens, and a picture of my favorite playwright, August Wilson.

With semicolons, it looks like this:

> On my desk, I always have a brand-new dictionary, which was invaluable when I was learning English—I buy a new one each year to see words that have recently come into English usage; at least one encyclopedia; a thesaurus, which helps me use more interesting words; pens; and a picture of my favorite playwright, August Wilson.

Look at one more example that includes long clauses and phrases in series and uses no semicolons:

> Acting as assistants to the world-famous cookbook writer, the chefs prepared the roasts, they cut the meat into long strips, they marinated these until the meat was coated, all the blood had drained out, and the feel of the meat became soft, they placed all strips into extremely hot pans with only a drop or two of olive oil, and the chefs then put each tender strip on a plate surrounded by some delicious vegetables.

That's a mouthful! It is much too complicated and definitely needs semicolons to separate each item in the series. (You could also break up these sentences with periods, but let's try using semicolons to see how the sentence would look using them.)

How many steps did it take to make the meal? Five steps, but one step has three procedures within it:

- preparation
- cutting
- marinating

1. meat was coated
2. meat had no blood
3. meat was soft

- meat put in pan
- strips placed on plates

Look at the sentence when it's punctuated properly with semicolons:

Acting as assistants to the world-famous cookbook writer, the chefs prepared the roasts; they cut the meat into long strips; they marinated these until the meat was tender, all the blood had drained out, and the feel of the meat became soft; they placed all strips into extremely hot pans with only a drop or two of olive oil; and the chefs then put each tender strip on a plate surrounded by some delicious vegetables.

EXERCISE II:

Use semicolons and commas to separate the series elements in the following sentences. Some sentences need both marks of punctuation, but some do not. You should use the existing punctuation in the sentences to help you understand how you should add semicolons and/or commas correctly. One sentence is correct as written.

Teacher's Note: These sentences can be fixed in various ways. Any answers that use the correct punctuation properly, even though they may be slightly different from those here, should be allowed.

1. In 1912, a gallon of gas cost only about $.12 a suit could be purchased for under $12.00 Henry Ford's invention, the Model-T automobile, went for under $1,000 and most homes sold for less than $10,000.

    In 1912, a gallon of gas cost only about $.12; a suit could be purchased for under $12.00; Henry Ford's invention, the Model-T automobile, went for under $1,000; and most homes cost less than $10,000.

2. Soon, merchants shopkeepers and wealthy landowners in Europe began collecting small parrots from South America. Amazon parrots rare Yellow-Winged parakeets and even some non-talking types of birds soon became hard to find in the wild.

   Soon, merchants, shopkeepers, and wealthy landowners in Europe began collecting small parrots from South America. Amazon parrots, rare Yellow-Winged parakeets, and even some non-talking types of birds soon became hard to find in the wild.

3. At the honors ceremony, the first speaker introduced Dr. Albert Jonson, the leader of the research team Paolo Martinez, who had volunteered as a test patient for the trials Delores Sklar, the person responsible for supplying the finances publicity and advertising and Dr. Maria Klaus, who reported the results to the media.

   At the honors ceremony, the first speaker introduced Dr. Albert Jonson, the leader of the research team; Paolo Martinez, who had volunteered as a test patient for the trials; Delores Sklar, the person responsible for supplying the finances, publicity, and advertising; and Dr. Maria Klaus, who reported the results to the media.

4. The report concluded that the school, suffering from a lack of donors, could not meet its obligations that the teachers would need to accept a pay cut that books would be used for an extra year that buses would be canceled and that there would be no sports teams for an entire year.

   The report concluded that the school, suffering from a lack of donors, could not meet its obligations; that the teachers would need to accept a pay cut; that books would be used for an extra year; that buses would be canceled; and that there would be no sports teams for an entire year.

5. Actors need to rely on more than their voices when on stage; they must reveal their characters through facial expressions, body language, and props.

    This sentence is correct as written.

6. Marine biology also includes the field of microbiology, the study of microscopic life chemistry, the examination of compounds in the ocean ichthyology, the study of fish and invertebrate anatomy, which deals with sea animals that have no backbones.

    Marine biology also includes the field of microbiology, the study of microscopic life; chemistry, the examination of compounds in the ocean; ichthyology, the study of fish; and invertebrate anatomy, which deals with sea animals that have no backbones.

7. We visited many tiny, but very interesting, unique, and old-fashioned cities on our trip: Rotorua, located near the Waikato River North Cape the town that is on the northern tip of New Zealand New Plymouth, which is on the east and Akaroa, near Christchurch on the South Island of the country.

    We visited many tiny, but very interesting, unique, and old-fashioned cities on our trip: Rotorua, located near the Waikato River; North Cape, the town that is on the northern tip of New Zealand; New Plymouth, which is on the east; and Akaroa, near Christchurch on the South Island of the country.

8. In the war movie, we saw many familiar and overused stereotypes: the cranky veteran who could teach the hero everything the young brave handsome hero who bragged too much the pilot who has never recovered from an accidental bombing and the wisecracking sergeant.

    In the war movie, we saw many familiar and overused stereotypes: the cranky veteran who could teach the hero everything; the young, brave, handsome hero who bragged too much; the pilot who has never recovered from an accidental bombing; and the wisecracking sergeant.

9. If you can master grammar usage punctuation and style, you're sure to get better grades in English.

    If you can master grammar, usage, punctuation, and style, you're sure to get an A in English.

10. After looking through the seed catalogue, we decided to order some lettuce, since we had had great success last year with it carrots, but not the yellow kind a variety of tomatoes, and two different kinds of peppers, one hot and one sweet.

    After looking through the seed catalogue, we decided to order some lettuce, since we had had great success last year with it; carrots, but not the yellow kind; a variety of tomatoes; and two different kinds of peppers, one hot and one sweet.

Parallelism in a Series

The items in each series that you have encountered have generally been the same part of speech and in the same form. This writing technique is called **parallelism**. Using parallel constructions makes your writing smoother and less jumpy. For instance, the series items in the following sentences are parallel:

- <u>Bears</u>, <u>chipmunks</u>, <u>rabbits</u>, and <u>foxes</u> are native to this forest. (all nouns used as subjects)
- Aiden <u>watches television</u>, <u>plays video games</u>, and <u>collects models</u>. (all verb phrases)

If the items in a series do not match in part of speech or form, we say that the sentence is not parallel. For example:

- At the animal shelter, dogs were <u>barking</u>, <u>running</u> around, and <u>slept</u>. (different verb tenses)
- Professional athletes should get large salaries because of <u>their intense training</u>, <u>they have short careers</u>, and <u>they are the ones who actually have amazing talents</u>. (1 prepositional phrase and 2 independent clauses)

You can correct the sentences by revising them in the following ways:

- At the animal shelter, dogs were barking, running around, and sleeping. (same verb tenses)
- Professional athletes should get large salaries because of their intense training, their short careers, and their amazing talents. (1 prepositional phrase with 3 nouns as objects)

   OR

   Professional athletes should get large salaries because they train intensively, have short careers, and have amazing talents. (3 verb phrases)

Almost any English construction can be used to make a series; you have already seen verbs, nouns, phrases, and entire clauses used this way. You have, we hope, learned how to punctuate them. All that's left is for you to keep them parallel.

In the following sentences, make all series items parallel. The sentences will need rewriting.

Teacher's Note: Many alternative solutions are possible. We have listed what could be considered the most logical, but students will come up with other correct sentences.

1. That two-year-old baby can walk, almost talking in complete sentences, and eats by himself.

    That two-year-old baby can walk, can almost talk in complete sentences, and can eat by himself.

2. The protesters tried to yell, waving signs, signed petitions, and, finally, marching down Main Street.

    The protesters tried yelling, waving signs, signing petitions, and, finally, marching down Main Street.

3. The members of the commission read the financial report, talked about its points, and the decision was made to invest in nuclear power.

    The members of the commission read the financial report, talked about its points, and made the decision to invest in nuclear power.

4. Having a good reputation is more important than the acquisition of money.

    Having a good reputation is more important than acquiring money.

5. The worst kinds of bosses are those who never listen, bullies, bad communication skills, and someone who insists on perfection.

    The worst kinds of bosses never listen, bully, communicate poorly, and insist on perfection.

6. I used to live in a city filled with tall buildings, the winds blew off the lake, and it was politically corrupt.

    I used to live in a city filled with tall buildings, blowing winds, and political corruption.

7. When Shaniqua was small, her dad prepared her for school, checking homework at night, and then allowing her to watch TV if she was receiving good grades.

    When Shaniqua was small, her dad prepared her for school, checked her homework at night, and allowed her to watch TV if she received good grades.

8. Washington was our first President: He was born in Virginia, being a great general, and the population elected him twice.

    Washington, our first President, was born in Virginia, was a great general, and was elected twice.

9. Everyone wanted to be like the most popular kid in the school, and some students began copying the way Dave walked, his clothing, and carrying their books in a plastic bag.

    Everyone wanted to be like the most popular kid in the school, and some students began copying the way Dave walked, the way he wore his clothes, and the way he carried his books in a plastic bag.

10. The house sitter had to prepare the meals, cleaning the house, and make sure the doors were locked.

    The house sitter had to prepare the meals, clean the house, and lock the doors.

Part III:
Show You Know

We hope that through the previous chapters, activities, and exercises, your words now say what you want them to, and your grammar and punctuation don't get in the way of your meaning. It's time to learn a few more punctuation rules that will improve your writing. Some common errors that many students make will hurt grades, applications, and writing in general. Even if the person reading your writing is able to figure out what you want to say, he or she may make a judgment about you if these errors are present.

Chapter One

Using Periods in Abbreviations

A period shows that a word has been abbreviated:

- They live at 29 Calvert Rd., Jackson, Mississippi.
- Mr. and Mrs. Hartford visited the U.N.
- Gen. Sun commanded the Korean military.

If a period that is used in an abbreviation comes at the end of a sentence, you do not need to add another period:

- Ray works for Sun Tan Products Unlimited, Inc.
- We traveled to Washington, D.C.
- The proper abbreviation for "teaspoon" is tsp.

If a period showing an abbreviation is *inside* the sentence, it is frequently, but not always, followed by a comma:

- Dr. Martin Luther King, Jr., began studying religion at an early age.
- My professor taught English, logic, Russian, etc., during her many years at the college.
- Henry will earn his M.D. next year.

Some abbreviations are so common, however, that no periods are used. Many words of this type, but not all, as you can see in the examples, are written in all capital letters:

- The FBI investigates crimes in the United States, but the CIA investigates international crimes.
- We received letters from CA, NY, and NM.
- The 25 mph speed limit lasted only two blocks.
- NASA recently launched three satellites.

Place a period after each abbreviation that needs one. Some abbreviations will not require a period. All punctuation that appears in the sentences should remain as it is. Use a dictionary if you need to identify whether some of the abbreviations do not need periods. One sentence is correct as written.

1. A crowd of kids always came down Grafton St at 8:00 am.

    A crowd of kids always came down Grafton St. at 8:00 a.m.

2. This letter has a postmark from the UK.

    This letter has a postmark from the U.K.

3. That NBC show was set in a law office in LA.

    That NBC show was set in a law office in L.A.

4. The tenants had to leave their apartments at 57 W Emery Ave; they couldn't afford the rents anymore.

    The tenants had to leave their apartments at 57 W. Emery Ave.; they couldn't afford the rents anymore.

5. People on the early shift work from 11:30 pm until 7:30 am.

    People on the early shift work from 11:30 p.m. until 7:30 a.m.

6. The Rev Albert Mahoney has been a minister since 1975.

    The Rev. Albert Mahoney has been a minister since 1975.

7. The FBI investigated the crime and solved it.

    Correct

8. Mr and Mrs L Grangerford invited friends to the New Year's Eve party.

    Mr. and Mrs. L. Grangerford invited friends to the New Year's Eve party.

9. Take Rte 49; then, turn left onto Martinique Blvd.

    Take Rte. 49; then, turn left onto Martinique Blvd.

10. Charles Barett Sr is the CEO of Walhyde Pharmaceuticals.

    Charles Barett, Sr., is the CEO of Walhyde Pharmaceuticals.

Chapter Two

Apostrophes

Generally, students think of **apostrophes** as difficult marks of punctuation to use correctly. However, apostrophes are not really much more complicated than the other punctuation marks.

An apostrophe has two functions:

- An apostrophe shows possession or ownership.
- An apostrophe shows that letters are missing from a word.

One thing that makes apostrophe use complicated is that there are many rules covering them. The easy part, though, is that the rules are not complicated.

The basic rule that everyone needs to know is that *you must not use an apostrophe to make words plural.* For example:

- Two *shoes*, not two *shoe's*
- Fifteen *pages* of notes, not fifteen *page's* of notes
- The *1990s*, not the *1990's*
- Summer vacation lasting two *months*, not two *month's*

A few cases are exceptions to this usage, however. To pluralize numbers and letters, you should use an apostrophe. For example:

- *A's* on your tests, not *As*
- Some Ford *150's*, not some Ford *150s*
- The four *i's* in Mississippi, not four *is* in Mississippi

Using Apostrophes to Show Possession

Rather than saying, "This is the book that belongs to Karen," you would normally say, "This is Karen's book." Instead of saying, "The note is for Kenny," most people would say, "It is Kenny's note." Both "Karen's" and "Kenny's" are possessives, as are the following words that contain apostrophes:

- *Lila's* prom dress (the dress belonging to Lila)
- *The oven's* buttons (the buttons belonging to the oven)

To make most singular words possessive, you simply add an apostrophe and an s. The toy belonging to a dog is a *dog's* toy, and a picture belonging to the President becomes the *President's* picture.

Take a look at the following list. These simple possessives are formed by adding an apostrophe s to the end of the word that shows the ownership:

Explanation	**Singular Possessive**
the car Henry has	Henry's car
the sound of a whistle	the whistle's sound
the shape of my desk	my desk's shape
the coins your father collects	your father's coin collection
the time that movie starts	the movie's start time
a hamster belonging to Dianna	Dianna's hamster
the smell in the basement	the basement's smell
the fuzzy picture on the television she watches	her television's fuzzy picture

But what about a singular word that ends in an *s*? These words use the same rule—add an apostrophe *s*. Some examples:

Explanation	**Singular Possessive**
the policies of one boss	a boss's policies
the system a business uses	the business's system
the shape of a glass	a glass's shape
the smell of one gas	a gas's smell
the house belonging to Mr. Williams	Mr. Williams's house
the grandchild of Tom Jones	Tom Jones's grandchild

When a word is plural; though, and ends in an *s*, only an apostrophe is added. Let's see how this rule applies to the previous examples when the Explanation column is pluralized:

Explanation	**Plural Possessive**
the policy of three bosses	three bosses' policy
the system a few businesses use	the businesses' system
the shape of many glasses	many glasses' shapes
the smell of more than one gas	the gasses' smell
the house belonging to the Williamses	the Williamses' house
the grandchild of the Joneses	the Joneses' grandchild

Some words are plural and do *not* end in *s*. For these, an apostrophe *s* must be added:

Explanation	**Plural Possessive**
the toys of two children	two children's toys
the religion those people believe in	those people's religion
the habitats of three fish	three fish's habitats
a decision by a group of men	the men's decision

Some words change their spelling when they go from singular to plural. The rules for showing possession, however, remain the same. If the plural does not end in *s*, add apostrophe *s*; if the plural does end in *s*, just add an apostrophe. For example:

Singular Possessive	**Plural Possessive**
a baby's clothes	the babies' clothes
a butterfly's wings	the butterflies' wings
an ox's duties	three oxen's duties
a wolf's tracks	a pack of wolves' tracks
a nucleus's shape	those nuclei's shapes

Here are some more examples of these rules:

Singular Noun	Possessive of Singular Noun
boy	boy's tie
fox	fox's meal
person	person's uncle
car	car's size
November	November's holidays
kite	kite's string
family	family's pet
dress	dress's collar
class	class's schedule
woman	woman's opinions
leaf	leaf's color
wolf	wolf's bite

Plural Noun	Possessive of Plural Noun
boys	the boys' game
foxes	the foxes' den
people	British and American people's language
cars	a million cars' sales
Novembers	the past two Novembers' weather
families	both our families' vacations
dresses	three dresses' costs
classes	all classes' schedules
women	a women's meeting
leaves	those leaves' colors
wolves	the wolves' territory

Teacher's Note: Emphasize to students that the pronunciation of the words that end in s's is not the important factor in punctuating them properly.

Determine what the correct plural, singular possessive, and plural possessive are for each of the words in the first column, and write your answers in the other columns. We have done two examples for you.

Singular	**Possessive**	**Plural**	**Plural Possessive**
boy	boy's	boys	boys'
princess	princess's	princesses	princesses'
1. month	month's	months	months'
2. dollar	dollar's	dollars	dollars'
3. James	James's	Jameses	Jameses'
4. giraffe	giraffe's	giraffes	giraffes'
5. lady	lady's	ladies	ladies'
6. goose	goose's	geese	geese's
7. hurricane	hurricane's	hurricanes	hurricanes'
8. mouse	mouse's	mice	mice's
9. century	century's	centuries	centuries'
10. box	box's	boxes'	boxes

If two or more people possess, own, or have something together, *only the last noun takes the apostrophe.* To describe the wedding of Romeo and Juliet, you would write, "Romeo and Juliet's wedding." If Luisa saw the new car that Gabe and his brother bought, you would show the possession like this: "Luisa saw Gabe and his brother's new car."

What happens, however, if two or more people own things individually? All the people take an apostrophe. For example, if Bob has a dog, and Josh has one, too, you would punctuate that ownership by writing, "Bob's and Josh's dogs." Toyota, Honda, and Nissan all make small trucks for the U.S. market, so in order to show that ownership, you would write, "Toyota's, Honda's, and Nissan's small trucks all sell in the U.S."

For apostrophe use in hyphenated words, put the apostrophe on the last noun, not the first. Therefore, the keys that your brother-in-law uses are your brother-in-law's keys.

Most pronouns do not take an apostrophe. "This pen is yours," *not* "This pen is your's." Some pronouns do need an apostrophe, though. If everyone in your class passed the test, you would write, "Everyone's grades were passing." Possessive pronouns are best learned by memorizing them. These use no apostrophes to show possession:

- My, your, his, hers, theirs, etc.

Apostrophes, however, are needed to show possession on some indefinite pronouns:

- Everyone's, everybody's, someone's, nobody's, etc.

EXERCISE II:

Put the apostrophe in the right place in each underlined word. Some words do not need any apostrophes because there is no possession, and some words that have apostrophes do not need them. Some sentences are correct as written.

1. Most people like <u>peanut butters</u> flavor more than sour <u>flavors</u>.

    peanut butter's; flavors is correct.

2. Angelo found the <u>pirates</u> treasure a few feet away from where they had buried it.

    pirates'

3. The team of doctors looked over all the <u>patients</u> charts and noticed that one <u>patients</u> disease was rare, but <u>everyones</u> symptoms were exactly the same.

    patients'; patient's; everyone's

4. <u>James</u> dream is to become a <u>doctors</u> assistant.

    James's; doctor's

5. Annie grabbed the <u>scissors handle's</u> and began cutting the wrapping paper.

    scissors'; handles

6. I believe that this <u>medicines</u> effect on my health has been very positive.

    medicine's

7. Twenty <u>cents</u> is just not enough to buy what <u>Ruth's</u> mom <u>wants</u>.

    Correct

8. When Naheed saw his <u>brothers jackets</u> hanging in the closet, he remembered that <u>Peter's</u> and <u>Georges</u> school had dismissed early that day.

    brothers'; jackets is correct; Peter; George's

9. Reporters for Channel Five <u>News</u> gathered around the <u>familys'</u> house.

    News is correct; family's

10. As more rain fell, the <u>grass</u> color changed from brown to green.

    grass's

11. The Greek <u>gods</u> home was on Mount <u>Olympus</u>.

    gods'; Olympus is correct.

12. I bought candy for last <u>weeks</u> party, but my twin <u>brother's</u> baby spilled most of it.

    week's; brother's is correct.

13. Ty eats <u>foods</u> with <u>lot's</u> of protein; this <u>builds</u> more <u>muscles</u>.

    foods, builds, and muscles are correct; lots

14. Those <u>books</u> <u>endings</u> are all the same: the <u>detective's</u> prove <u>everyones'</u> alibi is false.

    books'; endings is correct; detectives; everyone's

15. Grace has <u>hers</u>, but do you have <u>yours</u>?

    Correct

Using Apostrophes to Form Contractions

An apostrophe also shows that letters are missing from a word—this is called a contraction. For example:

- *I will* becomes *I'll*
- *They are* becomes *they're*
- *Should have* becomes *should've*
- *of the clock* becomes *o'clock*

The words with contractions in the sentences that follow are in italics. You could write, "I do not have any money" or "You are not going." If you were using less formal English, you might write, "I *don't* have any money" and "*You're* not going."

EXERCISE III:

Correct each of the following sentences and explain whether you made the correction because the word is a contraction, a plural, or a possessive.

1. Maurices cat got out last night.

   Maurice's; possessive

2. We almost forgot to put our table's back against the wall.

   tables; plural

3. Kala never listens to her mothers advice.

   mother's; possessive

4. Whats wrong with this picture?

   What's; contraction

5. The police were able to return the mans briefcase to him.

   man's; possessive

6. Someone put the bottles' of milk on the wrong shelf.

   bottles; plural

7. If you want to be a writer, youll have to accept that you will not get rich.

   you'll; contraction

8. Robin is a hard worker, but all the noises' outside her window distract her.

   noises; plural

9. The baby yawns even when shes not tired.

   she's; contraction

10. When we play hide-and-seek, Vickies always counting to fifty.

    Vickie's; contraction

11. The lights in the stadium were turned off at ten oclock.

    o'clock; contraction

12. Apple's get ripe in fall, so my friends and I pick them after school.

    Apples; plural

13. Im still here because I cant find Sharons birthday present.

    I'm and can't; contractions

    Sharon's; possessive

14. Luke asked the man sitting next to him why the store wasnt open.

    wasn't; contraction

15. Everybody loves it when Pat tells bad joke's.

    jokes; plural

The Difference Between *Its* and *It's*

When you add an *s* to the word *it*, do you need an apostrophe? Most of the time, an apostrophe shows that something belongs to someone:

- Sharon's purse is brand new. (the purse belonging to Sharon)
- This is Dexter's toy. (the toy belonging to Dexter)

But the word *its* is a special case. An apostrophe *s* on *it* can mean only one thing—an abbreviation of "it is." The word *it's* means "it is." Any other meaning is incorrect. Without an apostrophe, *its* means "belonging to it."

If you are unsure, test yourself by reading the sentence out loud, substituting "it is" for "it's." If the sentence makes sense, *it's* correct. Examples:

- It's my dog Duke. (*It is* Duke; correct)
- The dog lost *it's* way. (The dog lost *it is* way; incorrect)

This simple test should assure you that the word you use is correct.

EXERCISE IV:

Decide which form of the word belongs in the blank in each of the following sentences:

1. If **it's** sunny out, we're going swimming.

2. I immediately liked the restaurant for **its** cozy atmosphere.

3. The computer has been widely praised for **its** sleek design.

4. The meteor is moving fast, and **it's** headed right for my hometown.

5. Could you tell me when **it's** time for lunch?

Fill in the blanks in the following paragraph with *it's* or *its*:

Many Americans think that there are only four time zones in the Western hemisphere, but **6)** it's not that simple. For example, Nova Scotia has **7)** its own time zone, which is ahead of Eastern Standard Time. And some places do not observe Daylight Savings Time, so when **8)** it's one time in Arizona, another time is showing on clocks in Utah, even though the two states are in the same time zone. The country of Venezuela also observes **9)** its own time zone; **10)** It's half an hour ahead of the United States.

Chapter Three

Objective and Nominative Pronouns

A **pronoun** is a word that stands in for, or takes the place of, a noun. For example, look at the following sentence:

Lili took down the number so that she could call back later.
noun   **pronoun**

A **nominative pronoun** stands in for the subject of a sentence. An **objective pronoun** takes the place of the object in a sentence. The following is a list of some nominative and objective pronouns. Can you fill in the two that are left blank?

Nominative Pronoun	Objective Pronoun
I	me
he	him
she	her
we	<u>us</u>
<u>they</u>	them

Now let's see how these pronouns work in a sentence. What is the subject in the following sentences; in other words, what word performs the action?

1. I knocked Bert down.
2. I knocked him down.
3. He knocked me down.

The subject of sentence 1 is *I*. Bert is on the receiving end of the action—he is the *object* of the verb. In sentence 2, we use the objective pronoun *him* to stand for Bert. In sentence 3, the nominative pronoun *He* is the subject, and the objective pronoun *me* is part of the predicate.

Using the wrong objective pronoun probably will not prevent your reader from understanding what you mean. But if your reader isn't convinced that you know what you're doing as a writer, he or she probably won't believe much of what you're saying either.

We or *us*? *You* and *I*, or *You* and *me*? These and other pronouns can cause problems because they can be used as part of the subject of a sentence or as part of the predicate. Few people have trouble with using the correct pronoun in the subject. No one would say, for instance, "She am" or "I is."

If you understand the difference between nominative and objective pronouns, you will also know when to use *I* and when to use *me*:

- *I* is a nominative pronoun, and it's the subject of a sentence.
- *Me* is an objective pronoun, and it's in the object of a sentence.

People sometimes have trouble deciding whether to say "you and I" or "you and me." Ask yourself, "Do I want the subject or the object form of the pronoun?" Here's a sample sentence:

"You and I can wait here until the ferry comes back."

I is part of the subject of the sentence. If you took away the words *You and*, the sentence would read, "I can wait here until the ferry comes back." You certainly would not write or say, "Me can wait here until the ferry comes back." Therefore, you shouldn't write, "You and me can wait here until the ferry comes back."

Pronouns may also be objects of verbs or prepositions, and you need to know how to use them correctly in this position also. For example:

- Austin tagged me.
  Me is the object of the verb *tagged*. You wouldn't write, "Austin tagged I."
- Valerie handed the phone to me.
  Me is the object of the preposition *to*. You wouldn't write, "Valerie handed the phone to I."

Here are two more examples:

- This package is for you and <u>me</u>.
  Me is the object of the preposition *for*. You would not say, "This package is for <u>I</u>."
- Sarah invited you and her to the party.
  Her is the object of the verb *invited*. You wouldn't say, "Sarah invited <u>She</u> to the party."

From these examples, you can see that in sentences with multiple pronouns, one way to determine which to use is to say the sentence without one of the pronouns. This method won't work all the time, however, so you still need to understand the grammatical reasons behind your choice.

What about the words *we* and *us*? This choice works exactly the same as what we explained before. Is the pronoun part of the subject, the predicate, or does it function as an object? Then you'll know if it should be nominative or objective. Look at the following sentence:

<u>We</u> took turns watching the stove.

You wouldn't write or say, "<u>Us</u> took turns watching the stove." *We* is the subject, and, therefore, it is the nominative pronoun—it performs the action in a sentence.

Here are two more examples:

- The loud noise scared <u>us</u>.
  Us is the object of the verb *scared*. You know that "The loud noise scared <u>we</u>" is wrong, of course!
- Please accept this gift from <u>us</u>.
  Us is the object of the preposition *from*. "Please accept this gift from *we*" would be incorrect also.

In these two sentences, *us* is the objective pronoun—it takes the action of the verb or comes after a preposition.

Which of the following sentences is correct?

- <u>We</u> kids loved to go sledding in the winter.
- <u>Us</u> kids loved to go sledding in the winter.

The first sentence is right—*We* is the subject of the verb *loved*. Remove *kids* from both sentences, and you can easily see that the subject must be *we*. However, look at these two sentences:

- Things really looked bad for <u>we</u> nurses.
- Things really looked bad for <u>us</u> nurses.

Which one is correct, and how can you be sure? The second is the correct one. The pronoun is the object of the preposition *for*, so it needs to be objective. Using that logic, you can see that *us* is the correct pronoun.

Another way to figure it out is to take the word *nurses* out of the sentence. You get:

- Things really looked bad for <u>we</u>.
- Things really looked bad for <u>us</u>.

Now, let's look at two other pronouns that can be confusing: *they* or *them*.

They is the nominative pronoun. *Them* is the objective pronoun. Following the rules you learned about such pronouns, make a decision about which pronoun to use here:

"<u>They</u> and I ate lunch together."
OR
"<u>Them</u> and I ate lunch together."

The first is correct—both *they* and *I* are subjects of this sentence. On the other hand, when you place these words in the predicate or as objects of prepositions, things may seem more difficult. Just remember that *they* is only nominative, and *them* is only objective.

I gave <u>them</u> a present.
OR
I gave <u>they</u> a present.

That choice is obvious, and you instinctively know that the second sentence uses the wrong pronoun.

EXERCISE:

Circle the correct pronoun from each set inside the parentheses so that the sentences are correct.

1. You and (**I**, me) both know the number of council seats it will take for our party to win this election. Anyone who wants to take control of the government in this city is going to have to have the support of the firefighters' union. For instance, take the current Council President, Janice Watts. (**She**, Her) made sure she had the support of the firefighters early on. (**She**, Her) and the firefighters became friends; (**they**, them) went to many public events together. It may seem strange for (we, **us**) to be in the same political boat, but actually, (**we**, us) are a lot alike.

2. My brother was my best friend when I was growing up. Although times were tough for (he, **him**) and (**me**, I), (**we**, us) always stuck together. When my mom left (**us**, we), I could talk to (he, **him**). Later, though, when we were in high school, we started to drift apart. Lee went to college in New York, and I ended up in California. There were even a few years when I didn't speak to (**him**, he). Then, one day, suddenly, I got a call from Lee telling (**me**, I) that his first child had been born. It seems like things have come full circle; Lee and (me, **I**) seem like brothers again.

3. The doctor said (us, **we**) need to be on a low-fat diet. It had been a difficult decision for (she, **her**) and (**me**, I) to make, though. I made an appointment for (we, **us**) two to meet with a nutritionist. The next week, a date and time had been set for (we, **us**). Dr. Morrison, a certified expert in nutrition, told Sharon and (**I**, me) that there was nothing (**she**, her) could do to help (we, **us**) if we didn't change our eating habits. The doctor gave a list of allowable foods to (**I**, me) and a completely different list to (**her**, she). We both agreed to try to eat better; it would be good for (we, **us**) both to get our calories under control.

Chapter Four

Quotation Marks

Quotation marks are used in a variety of situations. The most common one is to enclose the words someone used. There are several rules for using punctuation with quotation marks:

The first rule is that a comma is used to lead into a quotation. The comma goes after the word which explains that something was said, exclaimed, yelled, whispered, etc.

- Hamlet said, "To be or not to be."
- Benjamin Franklin wrote in a letter, "A man wrapped up in himself makes a very small bundle."
- Keith stated, "You're late!" when I was early, so I knew he was joking.
- The police shouted, "Put your hands behind your head," but the suspect ran instead.
- My mom yelled, "Keep that radio down!"
- "Many people," Bart claimed, "are too greedy about money."
- "It's so hard to come up with things to write about," Emily sighed.

As you can see, *only the exact words* that were used take quotation marks around them. Ask yourself, "What exactly did Hamlet or Franklin or Keith or the police say?" The answer is enclosed by the quotation marks. My mom did not use the words "turn the radio lower." Her exact words are inside the quotation marks. Bart's exact words are shown, not just his idea. And Emily had a specific complaint that she used specific words to explain. We need the quotation marks to show people's words exactly as the words were used.

This brings us to the next important rule of quotation marks: Do *not* use quotation marks around indirect quotes or language:

- Marta was asked by her dad to shut the door.
- The coach told the players to be ready for some trick plays if they expected to win.
- Norm thought that some kinds of fish were poisonous.

In these three examples, the exact words are not in the sentences, and, therefore, no quotation marks are needed. Nobody said to Marta, "to shut the door"; the coach did not tell the players, "to be ready for some trick plays if they expected to win"; and Norm did not think to himself, "that some kinds of fish were poisonous."

EXERCISE I:

Take the three examples above and convert them to direct quotations, using proper punctuation and quotation marks.

Teacher's Note: Answers will vary somewhat from these possibilities, but make sure they are properly punctuated.

Marta's dad said to her, "Shut the door."

The coach told the players, "Be ready for some trick plays if you expect to win."

Norm thought, "Some kinds of fish are poisonous."

Many additional rules come into play when it comes to punctuating sentences that contain quotation marks. Generally, commas and periods go inside the quotation marks. Exclamation points and question marks that are part of the quote go inside the quotation marks; otherwise, they are outside. Here are some examples:

- "My computer," claimed Roberto, "makes my life easier."
- "I never stole anything in my life!" Barbara said.
- "Why did you cheat on that test?" asked the teacher.
- I wonder who asked, "Is there a straight road to paradise?"

Question marks, semicolons, exclamation points, and colons generally go outside the quotation marks, *unless they are part of the actual quotation*. Here are some examples. Notice the differences in punctuation between A's and B's:

A) Who said, "We can afford to lose"?
B) Josh said, "Why did we lose?"

A) Where were you when the teacher asked, "Whose book is this"?
B) The teacher asked, "Whose book is this?"

A) Karen said, "The answer is impossible to figure out"; she was wrong.
B) Karen said, "The answer is impossible to figure out; I'm confused."

A) Theresa had a lot of nerve when she said, "Joe did it"!
B) Theresa yelled out, "Joe did it!"

A) "Life, liberty, and the pursuit of happiness": This is the most famous part of The Declaration of Independence.
B) The most famous part of The Declaration of Independence is the phrase, "Life, liberty, and the pursuit of happiness."

Sometimes, you may want to have someone quote somebody else's words. In this case, you need to use what are called *single quotes*, which are made up of one quotation mark instead of two. The following are some examples of this important technique. We have bolded the single quotation marks so you can easily see the way they're used:

- The historian said, "One of John F. Kennedy's most common phrases was, **'**Let me say this about that.**'** "
- The astronaut explained that space was "empty, dark, and **'**the sound of silence**'** " seemed, in his words, "overwhelming."
- Dr. Robert said in his summary, " **'**Haste makes waste**'** is the opposite of **'**Nothing ventured, nothing gained.**'** "

You also use quotation marks to enclose titles of poems, short stories, chapter titles, song titles, essays, and words used in a special sense or for specific purposes:

- In Poe's "The Raven," the bird interrupts a man who is reading.
- "The Lottery" is one of the most frightening stories ever written.
- I always loved the older version of "Can't Get Over You."
- For some reason, the dog we bought that was advertised as a "best friend for infants" constantly barked at the baby.
- The word "taxes" is another way the government can control what people earn.

EXERCISE II:

Insert quotation marks and all necessary punctuation into the following sentences. For this exercise, all punctuation marks and capitalization that you see in the sentences are used properly, so you should leave these as they are. There are no single quotes in any of the sentences, and a few sentences are completely correct as they are.

1. Zena asked, How does the solar heater actually work

    Zena asked, "How does the solar heater actually work?"

2. How much, Yolanda wondered, is that car worth?

    "How much," Yolanda wondered, "is that car worth?"

3. Why didn't you enter that contest asked Jason

    "Why didn't you enter that contest?" asked Jason.

4. Mr. Johnstone said I am sure that this is the combination.

    Mr. Johnstone said, "I am sure that this is the combination."

5. The ball yelled the outfielder is stuck under the fence.

    "The ball," yelled the outfielder, "is stuck under the fence."

6. What a great taste and sweetness exclaimed the chocolate taster.

   "What a great taste and sweetness!" exclaimed the chocolate taster.

7. Didn't Caroline say, My water looks rusty

   Didn't Caroline say, "My water looks rusty"?

8. When did Shermaine comment that she loved to skate?

   Correct

9. The Beatles' song Yesterday is one of my favorites.

   The Beatles' song "Yesterday" is one of my favorites.

10. In the last book I read, there's a chapter called The Custom-House.

    In the last book I read, there's a chapter called "The Custom-House."

11. Daniel shouted, I won the lottery!

    Daniel shouted, "I won the lottery!"

12. California the Governor warned, has some economic challenges ahead.

    "California," the Governor warned, "has some economic challenges ahead."

13. The word immigrants is not mentioned on the Statue of Liberty.

    The word "immigrants" is not mentioned on the Statue of Liberty.

14. Have you read his poem called The Tyger

    Have you read his poem called "The Tyger"?

15. The salesman said You need to decide today; I told him that I needed more time

    The salesman said, "You need to decide today"; I told him that I needed more time.

16. What's the warranty on this here piece-of-junk TV were the words she used.

    "What's the warranty on this here piece-of-junk TV?" were the words she used.

17. The shout of Yay! echoed all over the field after we won the championship.

    The shout of "Yay!" echoed all over the field after we won the championship.

18. Did you ever see the modern version of *A Christmas Carol*?

    Correct

19. I wasn't sure that Gary said he couldn't be at the party.

    Correct

    OR

    It is possible that Gary was speaking about another person.

    I wasn't sure that Gary said, "He couldn't be at the party."

20. Ty complained, It just isn't fair!

    Ty complained, "It just isn't fair!"

Put quotation marks and all other punctuation marks where they belong. For this exercise, consider any other punctuation marks and capitalization in the sentences as correct. There are single quotes in many, but not all, of the sentences, and a few sentences are completely correct as written.

1. Did you mean to say evolution or heredity asked Julia.

   "Did you mean to say 'evolution' or 'heredity'?" asked Julia.

2. Bad excuses, like My dog ate my homework, are unacceptable

   Bad excuses, like "My dog ate my homework," are unacceptable.

3. Didn't I tell you, Don't do that! asked Connie's mom

   "Didn't I tell you, 'Don't do that!'?" asked Connie's mom.

4. I know who first used the quote that includes the phrase, fear itself.

   I know who first used the quote that includes the phrase, "fear itself."

5. That Senator said that in spite of what others do, she intended to vote against the bill.

   Correct

6. The manager explained to the crew, When you say I'll be on time, I expect you to.

   The manager explained to the crew, "When you say, 'I'll be on time,' I expect you to."

7. Maria asked What's the difference between your and you're?

   Maria asked, "What's the difference between 'your' and 'you're'?"

8. In the book, the monster couldn't speak; all it could do was grunt the word Kill!

   In the book, the monster couldn't speak; all it could do was grunt the word "Kill!"

9. When George W. Bush said, I misremembered, what he really meant to say was, I remembered incorrectly.

   When George W. Bush said, "I misremembered," what he really meant to say was, "I remembered incorrectly."

10. When did your boss ask you How long do you expect to work for this company

    When did your boss ask you, "How long do you expect to work for this company"?

11. Study the poem called Sunlight and Starlight and find a metaphor was written on the board the day the teacher was absent.

    "Study the poem called 'Sunlight and Starlight' and find a metaphor," was written on the board the day the teacher was absent.

12. Our driving teacher asked if we had read the chapter he had assigned.

    Correct

13. The band director said All members who received Congratulations! on their printed performance reviews are invited to the State Fair.

    The band director said, "All members who received 'Congratulations!' on their printed performance reviews are invited to the State Fair."

14. Look out the coach said for the rough spots on the field; I knew where they were already, though.

    "Look out," the coach said, "for the rough spots on the field"; I knew where they were already, though.

15. The speaker began with the words, My fellow Canadians, but then realized he was in the United States, so he paused, started over, and said, My fellow Canadians love the United States.

    The speaker began with the words, "My fellow Canadians," but then realized he was in the United States, so he paused, started over, and said, "My fellow Canadians love the United States."

Chapter Five

Commas

Earlier, we talked about using a **comma** with a conjunction to separate two independent clauses and using commas in a series. The comma is the most common punctuation mark in English and, probably, the most useful.

A comma is also used after a phrase or clause that begins a sentence:

- Before March, there usually aren't many flowers growing.
- First, we need to catch him.
- While Mel was patiently waiting for the sun to set that hot summer day, mosquitoes attacked him.
- To get to the baseball game on time, we had to leave three hours early because heavy traffic was expected.
- However, the TV was not fixed in time to watch the Super Bowl.
- No matter how hard Mr. Frederix and his family tried to catch them, the fish seemed not to be hungry that day.

Commas also separate items in a date or address from the rest of the sentence. Use a comma before and after elements of dates and addresses. Here are some examples:

- Ellen planted the apple tree on May 5, 2004, at her old house.
- Shakespeare was probably born on April 23, 1564, in Stratford-on-Avon.
- She moved to 65 Hilbert Terrace, Des Moines, Iowa, last year.
- The day the United States became involved in World War I was Sunday, December 7, 1941, when Japanese planes attacked Pearl Harbor, Hawaii.
- Friday, December 19, 2008, meant that only four shopping days remained until Christmas.
- Camden, New Jersey, is more than 2,390 miles from Los Angeles, California.

Place commas where they belong in the following sentences:

1. Until Jacob saw "Gone With the Wind" he didn't know what he wanted to be.

   Until Jacob saw "Gone With the Wind," he didn't know what he wanted to be.

2. My favorite restaurant is in Hyattsville Maryland.

   My favorite restaurant is in Hyattsville, Maryland.

3. Election Day was November 4 2008, only a short time before Thanksgiving.

   Election Day was November 4, 2008, only a short time before Thanksgiving.

4. After football season Lucas will have more time to study.

   After football season, Lucas will have more time to study.

5. During our trip to Johannesburg we made many friends.

   During our trip to Johannesburg, we made many friends.

6. On the other side of the city Mr. Stanfield was leaving for work.

   On the other side of the city, Mr. Stanfield was leaving for work.

7. A terrible headache had been bothering Trish since the morning she left Missoula Montana.

   A terrible headache had been bothering Trish since the morning she left Missoula, Montana.

8. Once the coach had them believing that they couldn't lose the football team quickly scored three touchdowns.

   Once the coach had them believing that they couldn't lose, the football team quickly scored three touchdowns.

9.   He had lived at 5944 Cedar Ave. Philadelphia PA until he was sixteen, but then he moved away.

He had lived at 5944 Cedar Ave., Philadelphia, PA, until he was sixteen, but then he moved away.

10.   Before the ceremony started the college president warned everyone to be polite.

Before the ceremony started, the college president warned everyone to be polite.

Commas are also used to separate contrasting elements in sentences and to avoid confusion. For example:

- There is water in that glass, not juice.
- Most scientists agree about the dangers of climate change, but not all.
- The more the child tried to understand the punishment, the less he could.
- The price of the game dropped one dollar, to $9.99.
- The next day, the man was fired.
- Soon after, Larry fell asleep.
- I prefer cookies to ice cream and hot fudge, and hamburgers to steak.
- Don't touch that, not even once!

EXERCISE II:

Place commas where necessary to avoid confusing sentences and to separate parts that are contrasting.

1.   Shawna wants to go to the mall not to go shopping but to socialize with her friends.

Shawna wants to go to the mall, not to go shopping, but to socialize with her friends.

2. Unlike other mammals platypuses lay eggs.

   Unlike other mammals, platypuses lay eggs.

3. This recipe uses powdered sugar not granulated.

   This recipe uses powdered sugar, not granulated.

4. Amelia hikes in the nature preserve but only on the weekends.

   Amelia hikes in the nature preserve, but only on the weekends.

5. Shortly after the Spanish Inquisition the Pope instituted a series of reforms.

   Shortly after the Spanish Inquisition, the Pope instituted a series of reforms.

6. Can you tell me how to get to the airport this time without consulting the GPS?

   Can you tell me how to get to the airport, this time without consulting the GPS?

7. Josef wants to go to the batting cages but needs to finish his essay.

   Josef wants to go to the batting cages, but needs to finish his essay.

8. The dictator stressed government for the people but not by the people.

   The dictator stressed government for the people, but not by the people.

9. The next week my supervisor missed the meeting.

   The next week, my supervisor missed the meeting.

10. Inside the room was really dark.

    Inside, the room was really dark.

Commas are needed when the writer needs to distinguish the parts of a sentence that modify and restrict a meaning from those that do not. While this may sound confusing, a few examples may help. In the following three sentences, which are without commas, the clauses to think about are *italicized*:

The principal gave an award to all children *who had participated in the race.*

Did the principal give an award to all the children in the school? Of course not. He gave awards only to kids who raced. The clause *who had participated in the race* modifies the word *children*; it restricts the meaning of *children*. In addition, it is a necessary part of the sentence: Take it out, and the sentence ("The principal gave an award to all children.") means that all children got awards.

Anyone *who contributed a thousand dollars or more* was invited to meet the Senator.

The same reasoning also works for this sentence. Not just *anyone* met the Senator, only big contributors.

The books *that I lent Terrence* have not been returned.

In this sentence, the clause, *that I lent Terrence*, is an essential part of the meaning. If it were missing, you could not understand the sentence correctly. The reader cannot know which books haven't been returned. The fact that I lent them to Terrence is essential.

"Commas are needed when the writer needs to distinguish the parts of a sentence *that modify and restrict a meaning* from those *that do not.*" This sentence is from the first paragraph of this section. You should notice that the italicized clauses are necessary to understand the meaning of the sentence; in fact, without the clauses, the sentence makes no sense at all. It would read, "Commas are needed when the writer needs to distinguish the parts of a sentence from those."

The four example sentences that you have gone over have modifiers that are called *restrictive clauses*, and they do not take commas around them. Notice how they contrast with the next three sample sentences. In these, the *italicized* clauses are *nonrestrictive*; they do not alter the basic meaning and are not essential to understand what is being said. This type of clause must have commas around it.

Viola's television *which has High Definition* uses much more electricity than her old one did.

What is the necessary information in this sentence? Is it that Viola's TV has High Definition or is it that the new TV uses more electricity? You understand that what is most important is that Viola's new TV uses more electricity. Therefore, the italicized clause does not affect the main idea of the sentence. It is *nonrestrictive*, and a nonrestrictive clause needs to be separated from the rest of the sentence by commas. The proper way to punctuate the sentence is:

Viola's television, which has High Definition, uses much more electricity than her old one did.

Abraham Lincoln *who freed all slaves* never imagined a black person's election to the Presidency.

Use the same logic for this sentence, and you can see that Lincoln's lack of ability to foresee Barack Obama's election is the main idea. It is common knowledge that Lincoln freed the slaves. That part of the sentence is another nonrestrictive clause, and it also needs commas around it. The proper way to punctuate the sentence is:

Abraham Lincoln, who freed all slaves, never imagined a black person's election to the Presidency.

The 1967 oil spill *which flooded the coastland* killed thousands of birds.

In this example, we know what oil spill the author is writing about because the sentence states that the spill occurred in 1967. The information in italics is just a supplementary fact. The most important part is that many birds were killed, not that the coast was flooded. The italicized part just adds material to the sentence, and it is, according to what has been explained, nonrestrictive. It takes commas around it to set it off from the rest of the sentence. The proper way to punctuate the sentence is:

The 1967 oil spill, which flooded the coastland, killed thousands of birds.

From these examples, you can see that the clauses all begin with a pronoun. Words to be alert for are *who, which,* or *that.* Restrictive and nonrestrictive constructions usually do begin this way. The pronoun is the word that should alert you to the possibility that a restrictive or nonrestrictive clause might be next.

EXERCISE III:

Place commas around all the nonrestrictive clauses in the following sentences. We have *italicized* the clauses for easier identification. Some of the clauses are restrictive and do act as modifiers. These do not need commas.

Teacher's Note: To extend the exercise, you could ask students to supply reasons for their exclusion or inclusion of commas.

1.   The anthropologist studied a past culture *that was ruled by women.*

The anthropologist studied a past culture that was ruled by women.

This is correct as is. The clause is restrictive, supplies necessary information, and cannot be removed without making the sentence lose its meaning.

2.   My advisor *who had contacted the admissions office* told me that I was *accepted to college.*

My advisor, who had contacted the admissions office, told me that I was accepted to college.

Commas show the nonrestrictive nature of the clause. The essential meaning of the sentence is not changed if the nonrestrictive clause is removed. The main thrust is that the advisor explained the student's acceptance to college, not the contact. The second clause is needed for the sentence to have any meaning. It cannot take commas.

3. That book *the one I left on the library table yesterday while studying* for *the test* has now been checked out.

    That book, the one I left on the library table yesterday while studying for the test, has now been checked out.

    The clause takes commas because it is unnecessary to the main meaning of the sentence. It is non-essential to understanding the sentence and merely adds extra information. It may be interesting, but it is nonrestrictive and needs commas.

4. King Marcus *who was the present king's grandfather* ruled Dominika for more than thirty years.

    King Marcus, who was the present king's grandfather, ruled Dominika for more than thirty years.

    The sentence's main thrust is that Marcus reigned for thirty years. The present king's being the grandson of Marcus is irrelevant, nonrestrictive and, therefore, must have commas.

5. People *who are considered "slaves to fashion"* are easy targets for designers of fancy clothing.

    People who are considered "slaves to fashion" are easy targets for designers of fancy clothing.

    The clause is essential, restrictive, and needs to remain in the sentence to get the whole meaning. Remove it, and the sentence would mean that all people, not just those who adore fashion, are easy targets. It takes no commas.

6. The latest jet *which is being planned at the present time* is twice as fast as a similar jet *that was built ten years ago.*

    The latest jet, which is being planned at the present time, is twice as fast as a similar jet that was built ten years ago.

The first clause needs commas because it is nonrestrictive and just offers some unimportant information. The essence of the sentence is that the newer jet is faster than the ten-year-old model. The last clause is absolutely necessary for the main meaning to be clear. No comma is needed.

7. People *who have never visited the United States* frequently want to go to Disneyland.

This is correct as is. The sentence cannot possibly mean that all people want to visit Disneyland, yet without the restrictive clause, it would mean exactly that.

8. Mark Twain *who was born in Missouri* left home to start working as a pilot on a Mississippi River steamer.

Mark Twain, who was born in Missouri, left home to start working as a pilot on a Mississippi River steamer.

The clause needs commas, as it is nonrestrictive and not essential to the main meaning of the sentence, which is that Twain worked as a pilot on a Mississippi River steamer.

9. Scientists *who are studying the deadly virus* rarely have time to work on other projects.

This is correct as is. Using the same logic as explained for number 7, the sentence with commas would mean that all scientists do not have time for other projects.

10. The balance sheets *which can explain the company's huge losses* mysteriously disappeared.

The balance sheets, which can explain the company's huge losses, mysteriously disappeared.

There must be commas around the nonrestrictive clause. Students may think that the "huge losses" are the most significant part of the sentence, but this is not the case. The information is not crucial to the sentence, which stresses that the balance sheets are no longer around. The clause is nonrestrictive and must have commas.

Underline all the clauses in the following sentences, using what you have learned so far in this chapter. For each clause, decide if it needs commas (non-restrictive) or does not need commas (restrictive). Some sentences are correct as written, some have no clauses for you to punctuate, and some have more than one clause. For this exercise, consider any other punctuation marks and capitalization in the sentences as correct.

1. Anyone who has ever seen a tornado closely never forgets it.

   This is correct as written. No commas are needed. The clause—who has ever seen a tornado closely—is restrictive.

2. The sky which is usually clear suddenly darkened.

   The sky, which is usually clear, suddenly darkened.

   Commas are needed; the clause is nonrestrictive.

3. The fourteenth amendment gives citizenship to all people who are born in the United States.

   This is correct as written. The clause—who are born in the United States—is restrictive and does not need commas.

4. Fortunately, the President listened to the warnings of his advisors who were the most able people around.

   Fortunately, the President listened to the warnings of his advisors, who were the most able people around.

   The clause beginning with "who" just adds information about the advisors. It is nonrestrictive and must have a comma before it.

5. When Charlotte gave her grandchildren their Christmas presents, they ignored the gifts which were a video game and a toy stove and immediately began playing with the box, using it as a fort.

   When Charlotte gave her grandchildren their Christmas presents, they ignored the gifts, <u>which were a video game and a toy stove</u>, and immediately began playing with the box, using it as a fort.

   Commas are needed; the clause is nonrestrictive.

6. Hundreds of the city's bells which were designed by a Swiss ironworker began to ring at the same time to celebrate the 500th anniversary of the town's beginning.

   Hundreds of the city's bells, <u>which were designed by a Swiss ironworker</u>, began to ring at the same time to celebrate the 500th anniversary of the town's beginning.

   Commas are needed; the clause is nonrestrictive.

7. The cake that you are baking will need more flour if you want it to taste good.

   The cake <u>that you are baking</u> will need more flour if you want it to taste good.

   No commas are needed. The clause—<u>that you are baking</u>— is restrictive.

8. Much of America's food that is canned or frozen could be produced naturally and organically which might be a bit more expensive.

   Much of America's food <u>that is canned or frozen</u> could be produced naturally and organically, <u>which might be a bit more expensive</u>.

   The first clause is restrictive and cannot take commas, but the second clause is nonrestrictive and needs a comma.

9. Pharmaceutical companies which want their drugs to be safe also spend billions of dollars researching anything that will improve the effectiveness of their products.

Pharmaceutical companies, <u>which want their drugs to be safe</u>, also spend billions of dollars researching anything <u>that will improve the effectiveness of their products</u>.

The first clause is nonrestrictive and needs commas. The second is restrictive and does not take a comma.

10. Eva Dasmonovitch who is Russia's top gymnast will probably win a gold medal in the next Olympics which will begin in three weeks.

Eva Dasmonovitch, <u>who is Russia's top gymnast</u>, will probably win a gold medal in the next Olympics, <u>which will begin in three weeks</u>.

Both clauses are nonrestrictive and need commas.

Chapter Six

Using the Right Verb Form

Look at the following two lists. You can see how the verbs change depending on who is doing something, and whether the "who" is singular or plural.

Example 1:

	Singular	**Plural**
First person	I run	We run
Second person	You run	You run
Third person	He runs, she runs, it runs	They run

Example 2:

	Singular	**Plural**
First person	I am	We are
Second person	You are	You are
Third person	He is, she is, it is	They are

Knowing how to use the forms of verbs correctly in your writing is another way of showing that you are in command of words. Earlier, you learned about the sequence of tenses and how to make sure that your verbs are in the proper tense. Now, you are ready to deal with the forms of verbs.

Some English verbs are **regular**. However, some are **irregular**.

Here are some regular verbs. They are called regular because they form the past tense by adding *d* or *ed*:

Present Tense	**Past Tense**
I bake	I baked
I look	I looked
I kick	I kicked

However, the English language also contains many irregular verbs; they take this name because they make their past tense without the *ed* on the end. Since irregular verbs are all different, their tenses are made in different ways. Here are a few irregular verbs:

Present Tense	**Past Tense**
I bring	I brought
I swim	I swam
I am	I was
I begin	I began
I steal	I stole
I catch	I caught
I bite	I bit
I think	I thought
I eat	I ate
I buy	I bought

EXERCISE:

Fill in the blanks in the following sentences by changing the form of the italicized verb or verbs supplied at the beginning of the sentence.

do
1. Last week, Tariq **did** his homework in only ten minutes.

take, bring
2. We **took** our dog to the vet, then we **brought** him home.

know
3. When Viki **knew** the club accepted her, she shouted for joy.

write
4. Yesterday, I **wrote** an email to the White House.

fall, stand
5. After she **fell**, the baby **stood** right up again.

go
6. Cameron **went** to last night's show at the music center.

run
7. I **ran** after the bus, but missed it and waited an extra hour.

ride
8. The last horse I **rode** was a beautiful brown color.

begin
9. Last month **began** on a Thursday.

grow, have
10. My tiny plant soon **grew** six feet tall, and we **had** juicy tomatoes all summer.

Chapter Seven

Subject-Verb Agreement

You know what a subject is. You know what a verb is. But did you know that they have to get along? In order for your subjects and verbs to be grammatically correct, they have to *agree*. But what does *agree* mean? It means that the actual subject of a sentence must be in the same singular or plural form as the verb is. In informal conversation, people do not always go by this rule, but it is an important one in formal writing.

You understand that the second sentence in each of the following pairs is the correct one and that the first one uses an incorrect verb:

Mom <u>are</u> looking for her glasses.   vs.   Mom <u>is</u> looking for her glasses.
subject verb   **subject verb**

Danny <u>am</u> sure he lost the dollar.   vs.   Danny <u>is</u> sure he lost the dollar.
subject verb   **subject verb**

Two <u>girls</u> <u>was</u> walking.   vs.   Two <u>girls</u> <u>were</u> walking.
    subject verb   **subject verb**

It's a little more complicated when the subject of the sentence is hidden, but, if you can figure out the exact subject, the rule about agreement still works.

<u>One</u> of the boys <u>were</u> running too fast.   vs   <u>One</u> of the boys <u>was</u> running.
subject   **verb**   **subject**   **verb**

In this sentence, how many boys were running too fast? The answer is that just one boy ran too fast. Therefore, you can see that the subject *One* is singular, and the verb *was* must agree with that singular subject.

There <u>are</u> only <u>one way</u> to do it   vs.   There <u>is</u> only <u>one way</u> to do it.

  verb   subject   **verb   subject**

The math problem can be solved in *only one way,* so the verb must agree with that *one way,* and it must be singular—*is.*

Correct each sentence by making the verbs agree with their subjects.

1. While Samantha take the pony back to the stable, Patrice are going to milk the cow.

   While Samantha takes the pony back to the stable, Patrice is going to milk the cow.

2. Although it were late, they was still hoping to win the race.

   Although it was late, they were still hoping to win the race.

3. Eric want to store the bags in the attic.

   Eric wants to store the bags in the attic.

4. I needs all of your paperwork before the company can finishes your taxes.

   I need all of your paperwork before the company can finish your taxes.

5. More stores is being built along the highway.

   More stores are being built along the highway.

6. Thirteen mice was part of the experiment.

   Thirteen mice were part of the experiment.

7. Only one of the teams from both regions were selected for the game.

   Only one of the teams from both regions was selected for the game.

8. History and mathematics is my favorite subjects.

   History and mathematics are my favorite subjects.

9. Everyone want a new car he or she can affords.

   Everyone wants a new car he or she can afford.

10. All parts of the game was returned to the store.

    All parts of the game were returned to the store.

A few of the sentences (most likely numbers 7-10) in the exercise may have been a bit difficult to figure out because you weren't sure which words actually made up the subject. There are a few additional ways of determining if the subject is singular or plural.

To make the designations easier to identify in the following examples, we abbreviated prepositional phrases with *PP* and *italicized* them; subjects are abbreviated by **Sub** in **bold**; and we underlined the verbs <u>V</u>. In addition, SING means singular, and PL stands for plural.

A subject is not found in a prepositional phrase. For example:

    All *of the girls* <u>catch</u> fish before **one** *of the boys* <u>catches</u> any.
    PL **Sub**   *PP*   <u>V</u>   SING **Sub** *PP*   SING <u>V</u>

    The **reasoning** *in the three essays* <u>was</u> important to Mr. Thompson.
       SING **Sub**   *PP*   SING <u>V</u>

Another placement of the subject that can cause problems is when there are two subjects joined by the word *or*. In these cases, the subject that comes *after* the *or* determines what the verb agrees with.

    The **flight instructor** *or* the **pilots** <u>sit</u> in the flight simulator.
       SING **Sub**   PL **Sub** <u>V</u>

    Either the **camels** *or* the albino **kangaroo** <u>is</u> around this turn.
       PL **Sub**   SING **Sub** <u>V</u>

Sometimes, modifying words come between the subject and its verb. Frequently these phrases are not relevant to the subject's being plural or singular. They are not the part of the subject that determines whether to use a singular or plural verb. You must recognize what the actual subject is in order to make it agree with the verb. The words in the examples are labeled as [*irrelevant.*] Notice that the words in brackets do not affect whether the subject is singular or plural.

The **President**, [*as well as his assistants,*] was ready for the announcement.
SING **Sub**   [*irrelevant*]   SING V

The five **members** [*of the city's best basketball teams, including Warren,*]
        PL **Sub**   [*irrelevant*]
were practicing.
    PL V

One hidden **clue**, [*located in the middle of his books,*] frequently points to
    SING **Sub**   [*irrelevant*]   SING V
the location of the treasure.

One problem that many students have is when a pronoun acts as the subject of a sentence, especially if the pronoun is **indefinite**. An indefinite pronoun is one that has no definite number to it. When this occurs, the writer needs to understand exactly what the pronoun means. Here are some guidelines:

Each	=	each one	Singular
Anyone	=	any single one	Singular
Everybody	=	every single person	Singular
Neither	=	neither one	Singular (usually)
None	=	not one	Singular (usually)

The other indefinite pronouns, *all, some, most,* etc., are plural.

Each *of the painters* wears the donated uniforms.
SING **Sub**   PP   SING V

None *of the noises* wakes me up at night.
SING **Sub**   PP   SING V

In a question, the subject usually breaks up the parts of the verb. Do not let this confuse you. All you need to do is change the question to a statement and then the subject and verb will reveal themselves. The rules for subject-verb agreement can then be applied.

<u>Does</u> **each person** <u>hope</u> to win the lottery?
SING <u>V</u>   SING **Sub**   <u>V</u>

Each person <u>does hope</u> to win the lottery.
   SING **Sub**   SING <u>V</u>

<u>Do</u> **Joan and Thomas** <u>hope</u> to win the lottery?
SING <u>V</u>   SING **Sub**   <u>V</u>

Joan and Thomas <u>do hope</u> to win the lottery.
   SING **Sub**   SING <u>V</u>

EXERCISE II:

Correct all subject-verb agreement issues in the following sentences by fixing the incorrect verbs; use the subjects as they appear in the sentences. A few are correct as written.

1.   One of the wild animals on the African Plains are related to kangaroos.

     One of the wild animals on the African Plains is related to kangaroos.

2.   Everyone with a set of A's on the earlier papers do not need to take the test.

     Everyone with a set of A's on the earlier papers does not need to take the test.

3.   How does Helena and Maria play field hockey so well?

     How do Helena and Maria play field hockey so well?

4.   All of the book need to be read by tomorrow.

     All of the book needs to be read by tomorrow.

5. Either the TV or the computers has to be turned off.

    Either the TV or the computers have to be turned off.

6. The people in costume, including Grams, PopPop, and Gramps, are at the movies.

    Correct

7. That calendar and the pictures, the ones I bought for the holiday, is not wrapped yet.

    That calendar and the pictures, the ones I bought for the holiday, are not wrapped yet.

8. Three issues of that comic book or just one rare edition of the other cost $100.

    Three issues of that comic book or just one rare edition of the other costs $100.

9. Nobody eats that because it smells horrible!

    Correct

10. Each parent walk through the security fence before all the children do.

    Each parent walks through the security fence before all the children do.

11. Are the children's dog covered up for the freezing weather?

    Is the children's dog covered up for the freezing weather?

12. The book in your hands are brand new, so keep it covered.

    The book in your hands is brand new, so keep it covered.

13. She and her brother walks past my house every day.

    She and her brother walk past my house every day.

14. Three students in my class, including Bev, has won scholarships.

    Three students in my class, including Bev, have won scholarships.

15. It seems that Carol's main interest in life are rock singers.

    It seems that Carol's main interest in life is rock singers.

Part IV:
Commonly Confused Words

Since you want to make a good impression on your reader, you'll want to be extra-careful to use the right word. If two words sound alike, and if you misuse one of these words for the other, it can affect your grade. Your computer's Spell-Check won't understand which word you need to use, so you need to understand the difference between these words that sound alike, but have different meanings.

Teacher's Note: We recognize that the frequency of these commonly confused words varies greatly and that there are many more than the sixteen listed. However, the first four discussed are the ones that are most often misused, which is why there are extensive exercises covering them. The remaining words are, however, well-represented in the culminating exercise and in the activity.

Your and *You're*

The word *your* always means "belonging to you":

- One of *your* shoes is untied.
- *Your* favorite holiday is Christmas.
- I have *your* test results.

In contrast, the word *you're* is a contraction of, and *always* means, "you are." It has no other meaning:

- I just heard that *you're* running for office!
- *You're* not really going to wear that suit, are you?
- Jeremy said to Helene, "*You're* beautiful."

Make sure you distinguish between the two spellings in your writing.

EXERCISE I:

Read each of the following sentences and fill in the blank(s) with either *your* or *you're*.

1. Did you really think **you're** funny?

2. It's hard to get **your** homework done when **you're** sleepy.

3. **You're** going to make some really good friends at **your** new school.

4. Make sure you pick up **your** blue ribbon on **your** way out.

5. I know that **you're** all going to the Prom, but I don't know how **you're** getting there.

6. "**Your** performance was simply stunning!" cried Elsa to the dancer.

7. "I've seen a lot of cases like this," said Doctor Viello. "**You're** going to be just fine."

8. "Whenever people hurt **your** feelings, try to forgive them," my mom advised me.

9. "Because of a problem with the heating system, class has been cancelled," announced the principal. "**You're** all dismissed for the day."

10. As soon as I sat down at my desk, Jenny asked me, "How was **your** vacation?"

To, Too, and *Two*

To is a preposition:

- Tricia is going *to* the wrestling match.
- Put the pedal *to* the metal!
- He took the book *to* the library.

To also goes with verbs to make what are called infinitives:

to catch
to take
to see
to want
etc.

- *To* learn about the Spanish-American War was the assignment.
- Misha is trying *to* understand the math problem.
- We wanted *to* wait for the bus.

Too means "also" or "in addition":

- Danielle likes baseball, but she likes dancing, *too*.
- I'll put the cheese in the basket, *too*.
- Is Johann going, *too*?

Too is also an adverb that means "very" or "overly":

- This bag is a little *too* orange for me.
- Don't talk *too* loudly while everyone is still asleep.
- There were *too* many players on the field.

Two is the number that's one more than one:

- At *two* minutes after twelve, we got the news.
- *Two* years ago, the team won the championship.
- We have *two* dogs.

EXERCISE II:

Read each of the following sentences and fill in the blank(s) with either *to*, *too*, or *two*.

1. Bernard is going **to** soccer practice.

2. Naomi is going **to** be late.

3. There are **too** many kids in your class.

4. The baseball team needs a good pitcher, but the other players are important, **too**.

5. More than **two** people are allowed to ride the roller coaster today.

6. It looks like we take this bridge to get **to** New Jersey.

7. Someone is listening **to** music in the other room.

8. To get the right answer, you have **to** divide by **two**.

9. Nobody wanted **to** volunteer for the job.

10. It is good **to** give, but we like receiving, **too**!

11. The **two** major companies have merged **to** become one corporation.

12. Liam decided he was **too** cool to be seen with his **two** little sisters.

13. Are you going **to** cheer me on tonight?

14. We can't decide who is right, so we've decided **to** put the question **to** our principal.

15. **To** give that speech, Kelley prepared for **two** hours, in addition **to** doing her regular homework.

Their, They're, and There

Their is a possessive pronoun meaning "belonging to them":

- Susan and Paul named *their* dog Stewart.
- *Their* puppy was very active.
- They took Stewart to *their* vet for shots.

They're is simply a contraction of *they are*:

- *They're* trying to understand what went wrong.
- Where do you think *they're* going?
- I was surprised *they're* here so early.

If you are trying to figure out whether to use *they're*, say the sentence out loud using "they are" in it.

They're going to buy a new computer. = *They are* going to buy a new computer.

Finally, *there* has two uses:

It is an adverb that tells the location of something:

- Please put the grocery bags *there*.
- I left my coffee cup right *there*, and now it's gone!
- He is *there* now.

It also begins certain sentences or clauses, as when you say:

- *There* are no more green shirts; you can have a red one or a blue one.
- *There* might be a collar on the dog we found.
- I am trying to find out if *there* is money in the cash register.

EXERCISE III:

Read each of the following sentences and fill in the blank(s) with either *their*, *they're*, or *there*.

1. Both speakers spilled **their** coffee when they heard the loud noise.

2. Gwen says she and Michelle can't come to the reception party, but **they're** going to be at the wedding.

3. What is the weird-looking metal globe over **there**?

4. The best thing about these pots and pans is that **they're** so easy to clean.

5. Did you put the commas where **they're** supposed to go?

6. When the candidates walked onstage, I immediately noticed **their** beautiful ties.

7. Kyla has called home twice, but **there** was nobody **there**.

8. Before the guests leave, make sure you get **their** names.

9. When **there** is a break in the show, the audience members can stand and stretch **their** legs.

10. **There** is no doubt that **they're** the ones who caused this mess.

Affect and Effect

After the previous three common errors, the words that are most frequently used for one another are **affect** and **effect**. They seem as if they could almost mean the same thing, but they are very different.

Affect is a verb, and nothing else. It means "to have an influence on" or "to cause to happen":

- How did the flu *affect* your studying?
- The temperature *affected* the roads so much that they froze.
- Taking one species of animal out of its habitat will *affect* the whole ecosystem.

Effect is primarily a noun. It means "a result or accomplishment." Notice the sample sentences that follow:

- What *effect* did the flu have on your studying?
- One *effect* of the cold temperatures was that the roads froze.
- Removing all earthworms from the ground caused an *effect* the scientists didn't expect.

Effect also means "a state of readiness":

The skateboarding law goes into *effect* next week.

Accept and Except

The word **accept** means "to receive willingly," "to take in payment," or "to make a favorable reply":

- Will you please *accept* this gift?
- We *accept* only credit cards.
- Herb *accepts* his responsibility for the mistake.

The word **except**, however, means "but" or "with this exclusion":

- Everyone went to the party *except* Barry.
- There's no way to that island, *except* by boat.

Advise and Advice

Advise is a verb that means "to offer information or opinion," and *advice* is a noun that refers to the information that is given:

- I was able to *advise* my son about college.
- I gave him some *advice* on which college to attend.

Already and All Ready

The first word, *already*, means "by this time" or "previously":

- He has *already* finished the work.
- Louisa had *already* left by that time.

The words *all ready* indicate that something is completed, completely prepared or ready:

- We were *all ready* for the music.
- When I put my shoes on, I'll be *all ready*.

Allusion and Illusion

These two should be easy to use properly because they are very different and have only one use.

An *allusion* is a reference to something else:

- Teri made an *allusion* to Stephen King's book in her paper.
- The *allusion* to nuclear physics was too odd for me to understand.

An *illusion* is a hallucination, a trick, something that is not real, or something that misleads:

- We saw an *illusion*—a drawing that changed from a car into a face.
- The magician's *illusion* of making an elephant disappear was incredible.

Altar and Alter

These two words should also be easy to use correctly.

The first one, alt**a**r, is a noun that means a "a raised platform for performing religious rituals":

- The priest stood next to the *altar* for the blessings.
- Many prisoners were sacrificed on the *altar* of the Aztec gods.

The second word, alt**e**r, is a verb that means "to change or fix":

- The tailor had to *alter* the dress before the wedding.
- Nothing could *alter* the spoiled kid's behavior.

Capitol and Capital

*Capit**ol*** refers *only* to a government place or building:

- We visited the *Capitol* in Washington and watched the Senators arrive.
- Is the *capitol* building in your state open on Thanksgiving?

All other meanings use the word *Capit**al***:

- Use a *capital* "G" on that word.
- What's the *capital* of Georgia?
- Murder is a *capital* crime.
- Do you have any *capital* to invest?

Principle and Principal

Here is another easy one. The first word, *princi**ple*** means "a law, rule, or code of behavior":

- Try to live by honest and fair *principles*.
- The most basic *principle* is to treat others as you want to be treated.

*Princi**pal*** has a few meanings, though:

- the person in charge of a school:
  The *principal* sets up the school schedule.

- someone or something that is most important:
  The *principal* reason for driving a small car is to reduce CO_2 emissions.

- money:
  The *principal* plus the interest we owe will total over $50,000.

Coarse and Course

You may already know the differences between these two words, but if you don't, they're easy to remember.

Coarse means "rough, not smooth"; this word can refer to the feel of something, or it can be used to describe behavior:

- That dress was too *coarse* to be comfortable.
- Kendra used some *coarse* language to describe her ex-friend.

Course, of course, refers to:

an ordered path
a progression in school or a subject
a part of a meal

- The *course* they took was wrong, and they arrived late.
- What *courses* do you need to graduate?
- The last *course* was dessert.

Lose and Loose

These two words are mixed up all the time, but they certainly do not need to be, since they are very different.

Lose means the opposite of "to win" and the opposite of "to find" or "to gain." It also means "to be defeated":

- Jermain didn't *lose* his position on the baseball team.
- How could you *lose* your keys again?
- It was obvious that we were going to *lose* another day when the plane was delayed.
- I don't know how we could *lose* to that team!

But *loose* has only one major meaning—"not tight":

- The pants were much too *loose* for him to wear.
- You need to stay *loose* and not freeze up when Mr. Patrick calls on you.

Weather and Whether

We're pretty sure that you know these two words, but just to reinforce the meanings, here is the difference.

Weather refers to the conditions outside, such as rain, wind, temperature, etc.:

- The rainy *weather* made us decide to stay home.
- Our *weather* this summer has been just great!

Whether refers to possible alternatives; it's a word that shows different possibilities:

- Nyeri wasn't sure *whether* to stay at the bus stop or catch a cab.
- Do you know *whether* Luke is singing at the club tonight?

Angel and Angle

The next two words in this section are these two that are simply mixed up because of spelling.

An *angel* is a spiritual or heavenly creature. It can also be a term that shows affection:

- Do you believe in *angels*?
- According to the Bible, the *angel* Gabriel announced the birth of Jesus.
- "You're my *angel*," the mother said to her little boy after he behaved well at the store.

An *angle* means "a corner" or "a position":

- How do you calculate the *angle* so that the room is the right size?
- He had a great *angle*, so he could see the horses during the whole race.

Passed and *Past*

The final two words in the section are the verb *passed* and the word *past*, which can be a noun or an adjective. Inexperienced or careless writers sometimes mix these two up and use them for one another. Their differences are very easy to understand, however.

The word *passed* has only one meaning and use. It's used to show that something has happened or has occurred. It is the past tense of the verb *to pass*:

- You *passed* your driving test.
- Halloween *passed* last year with very few trick or treaters.

The word *past*, on the other hand, refers to time that has already happened. It also means "beyond." *Past* can also be an adjective meaning "ago:"

- In the *past*, you believed in Santa Claus.
- We drove *past* the crowded mall.
- Lee remembered years *past*, before he had met Jordan.

EXERCISE IV:

For each of the following sentences, circle the right word from the pairs of commonly confused words so that the sentence is correct.

1. Marc's clothing was too (lose, **loose**) after he came back from the hospital.

2. I don't even care (**whether,** weather) you go!

3. I thought that my girlfriend was so beautiful that she resembled an (angle, **angel**).

4. One (**principle,** principal) I'll never forget is to help people who are homeless.

5. No one could get (**past,** passed) the guards.

6. I could never (except, **accept**) the idea of terrorism to achieve goals.

7. (Too, **To**, Two) get (too, **to**, two) the restaurant, turn left in (too, to, **two**) blocks.

8. Sacramento is the (capitol, **capital**) of California.

9. (**You're**, Your) bothering me.

10. Don't (loose, **lose**) the directions, or we will have to (altar, **alter**) our plans.

11. Park your car over (**there**, their, they're) because (there, **their**, they're) car is in (**you're, your**) usual spot.

12. That dog sure has (**coarse**, course) fur. (It's, **Its**) collar is missing, (**too**, to, two).

13. Can you (advice, **advise**) me about which car I should buy?

14. The golf (coarse, **course**) was always empty, which was sure to (effect, **affect**) the city's finances.

15. My (principals, **principles**) on cruelty to animals will not change.

16. The game had (all ready, **already**) started.

17. I (**passed**, past) an accident on my way to see the (**Capitol**, capital) building.

18. Please explain (**your**, you're) (illusion, **allusion**) to Shakespeare more clearly.

19. (**Except**, Accept) for the vegetables, which were overcooked, the meal was delicious.

20. What (**effect**, affect) did the terrible (whether, **weather**) have on the fishing?

21. We were finally (<u>already,</u> **all ready**) for the parade.

22. (<u>There, Their,</u> **They're**) not (**too,** <u>to, two</u>) tight; in fact, the pants are (<u>lose,</u> **loose**).

23. Beautiful flowers were placed on the (**altar,** <u>alter</u>) next to a statue of a small (**angel,** <u>angle</u>).

24. Give me some (<u>advise,</u> **advice**) on how not to (<u>loose,</u> **lose**) my place in line.

25. Our (**principal,** <u>principle</u>) told the graduating class, "Whatever (**your,** <u>you're</u>) goals are, you must work to achieve them."

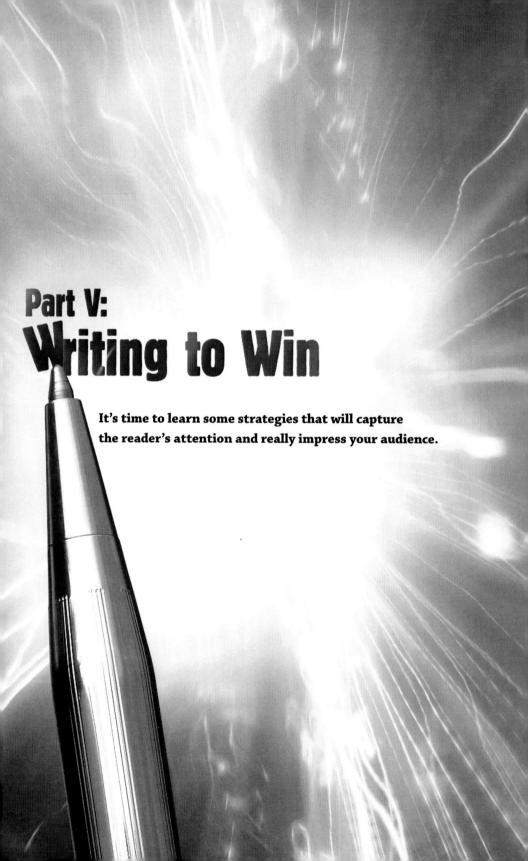

Part V:
Writing to Win

It's time to learn some strategies that will capture
the reader's attention and really impress your audience.

Chapter One

Active Voice

In this section, you will be working on making writing clear, direct, and powerful. Therefore, we need to discuss a technique called the **active voice**. Every English verb is in either the *active* or the **passive voice**. One of the best ways to understand what this means is through examples:

Active Voice	**Passive Voice**
kicked	was kicked
took	was taken
loves	is loved

You can see that the active voice is direct. It connects the subject with the verb directly:

- I kicked the ball.
- I took the money.
- He loves the puppy.

The passive voice puts the subject—the person or thing performing the action—after the verb. The subject is separated from the verb:

- The ball was kicked by me.
- The money was taken by me.
- The puppy is loved by him.

In some passive voice sentences, however, there is no subject mentioned:

- The ball was kicked.
- The money was taken.
- The puppy is loved.

Why should you avoid the passive voice? For one thing, it adds words to your sentence. When you put the subject last, you have to add a minimum of two words: a helping verb like *is* or *was*, and a helping preposition like *by*:

- The form is stamped by the manager. vs. The manager stamps the form.
- Refunds will be given by the theater. vs. The theater will give refunds.
- The butter was spread by Oliver. vs. Oliver spread the butter.

The passive voice also gives the writer the possibility of leaving off the subject entirely. Many times, politicians use the passive voice, as this wording does not implicate them in something negative. Passive voice is useful if you want to avoid responsibility for something, as in the following statements:

- Mistakes were made.   vs. I made mistakes.
- The car was crashed yesterday. vs. I crashed the car yesterday.
- The enemy is not defeated.   vs. We have not defeated the enemy.

But the most important reason to use the passive voice sparingly is that it makes your reader wait for the subject of the sentence. For instance, read the following sentence:

Amazing new sounds on the drum machine continue to be invented by Kay-T, a wild genius.

The subject, "Kay-T," comes close to the end of the sentence; you have to read almost to the end before you know who is creating these "amazing sounds." Now read the sentence in the active voice:

Kay-T, a wild genius, continues to invent amazing new sounds on the drum machine.

You don't have to wait at all to understand who is performing the action. The subject connects almost immediately with the verb, as opposed to the passive voice sentence, in which both subject and verb come near the end.

Finding the passive voice in your own writing and transforming it into the active voice will make you sound—and maybe feel—more powerful and confident. Converting passive to active is not just a matter of one-to-one switching of words; it's also one of rewording the sentence to achieve its full impact. Rewriting sentences in the active voice will require some thinking about how you want your sentence to read.

Which sentence of these two pairs has the most power? Why?

- People were stricken by cholera. vs. People caught cholera.
- Britain was defeated by Spain. vs. Britain lost to Spain.

Here is a longer sentence that includes two examples of the passive voice. Notice how much more powerful the active voice is:

Nuclear secrets were sold to the Communists nearly every day by the spy who was convicted by the U. S. government.

vs.

The U. S. government convicted a spy who sold nuclear secrets to the Communists nearly every day.

Remember: Your verbs deserve the active voice.
(!)

Not every sentence, though, should take the active voice. Many work better in passive voice. It depends on the effect the writer wants to create, and some sentences can achieve their purpose by actually employing the passive voice. Writers may want to delay introduction of the subject until later for effect. Look at these two sentences:

- The recipe was carefully guarded by generations of our family.
- Generations of our family guarded the recipe.

The active voice sentence eliminates three words and gets to the point more quickly. However, the author of this sentence may have wanted to emphasize that the family did the work of keeping the recipe secret. If so, the passive voice works more effectively. Another example:

A) Every Tuesday, Mr. Gregory's huge lawn had to be hand-mowed by Frank.

The active voice (A) would be more traditional, but if the writer's intent was to point out that the difficult job belongs to Frank, this sentence in the passive voice (B) works better.

B) Frank had to hand-mow Mr. Gregory's huge lawn every Tuesday.

Sentence B does not have the same emphasis as Sentence A does. In B, the active voice sentence, the main idea is that Tuesdays were the day to do the job.

In the passive voice sentence that follows, the emphasis is on the mummies, but in the active voice sentence, the writer places the country at the center of focus:

Passive Voice		**Active Voice**
Mummies were rarely displayed in Egypt.	vs.	Egypt rarely displayed mummies.

Sentences like these two, however, might very well sound better in the passive voice, as it adds some mystery:

Passive Voice		**Active Voice**
The screen was left open last night.	vs.	He left the screen open last night.
Page 21 had been cut out by someone.	vs.	Someone cut out page 21.

So, to summarize: Use the active voice most of the time, but, in some cases, the passive voice works better. It depends on what *you want* to say.

Change the verbs in the following sentences from the passive voice to the active voice, or vice versa. Be prepared to explain which sentence of each pair is better. It will be necessary to reword some of the passive voice sentences by adding subjects. Some of the revised passive voice sentences may sound awkward, which should be another indication to you that sentences written in the passive voice should not be your main way of expressing yourself.

Teacher's Note: Students' explanations for why they prefer one sentence over another will vary throughout.

1. The donut was chewed by Roger.

    Passive voice. Roger chewed the donut.

2. Opera is frequently enjoyed as a cultural event.

    Passive voice. Nadine enjoys opera as a cultural event.

3. Until Mom called out, "Dinnertime!" Mike and Lashawn played video games.

    Active voice. "Dinnertime!" was called out by Mom, but video games were being played by Mike and Lashawn.

4. The temple was built by peasants.

    Passive voice. Peasants built the temple.

5. Geena put a lot of thought into the planning of the wedding.

    Active voice. A lot of thought was put into the planning of the wedding by Geena.

6. Denise listened to the music.

    Active voice. The music was listened to by Denise.

7. This sculpture is being worked on.

   Passive voice. Nathan is working on this sculpture.

8. There is no evidence found by detectives that any windows were broken by the suspect.

   Passive voice. The detectives found no evidence that the suspect broke any windows.

9. The hands of the clock will be turned by the curator of the museum.

   Passive voice. The curator of the museum will turn the hands of the clock.

10. If the company drills for oil, it could make a lot of money.

    Active voice. If oil is drilled for by the company, a lot of money could be made.

11. The breakfast was cooked by my five-year-old niece.

    Passive voice. My five-year-old niece cooked breakfast.

12. The writer's style was admired by all her fans.

    Passive voice. All the writer's fans admired her style.

13. Tim's shoulder was broken by the fall.

    Passive voice. The fall broke Tim's shoulder.

14. A police officer stops Laura for speeding.

    Active voice. Laura is stopped by a police officer for speeding.

15. The team will surely be stumped by the question in the final round.

    Passive voice. The question in the final round will surely stump the team.

Chapter Two
Word Choice

Mark Twain wrote, "The difference between the right word and almost the right word is the difference between lightning and the lightning bug." Writers understand this huge difference. You should understand it also. For example, if you want to describe Clark as a smart student, saying that he is "very, very, very smart" is not as effective as calling him "brilliant" or "a genius."

In this chapter, we will discuss how to decide on the right word.

Many times, the wrong word is used because you don't take the time to think about revising your writing. The following are examples of wrong word choice:

- using a word that sounds like the one you want, but has a slightly different meaning
- choosing a synonym that is too difficult or formal
- using a slang or informal word in formal writing
- leaving out a word
- using clichés
- using filler words
- writing with unnecessary repetition

Read the following paragraph that was submitted in an English class:

In August in the year 2007, the I-35 bridge in Minneapolis collapsed. Thirteen people were killed in the terrible tragedy. Many more folks were wounded, and the rest of their lives were shot. Experts found that the cause of the bridge collapse was basically the age of it. The NTSB investigated the collapse and said that the gusset plates on the bridge were not powerful enough to support the number of traffic on the bridge. They should have been stronger. In other words, when the structure was built, there were not as many cars going over it. As traffic got more, the bridge got weaker. In addition, an extra load of weight was on the bridge from construction equipment. In fact, this may be a growing problem.

What are some things that make this passage confusing and poorly written?

- This paragraph uses filler words and phrases like *basically, in other words,* and *in fact.*
- Some of the phrasing is redundant: Wouldn't "In August, 2007," sound better than, "In August in the year 2007"?
- The word *collapse* is used three times in one short paragraph. The author should think of different ways to refer to this subject. Words like *accident, failure, shatter,* etc., would make the paragraph more interesting.
- The clichés *folks* and *lives were shot* do not belong in a formal paper; even if this were not formal English, these phrases are slang usages and are out of place in a paragraph that deals with death and destruction.
- The author should have made some different word choices in the paragraph. The word *wounded* is a synonym for *injured,* but it doesn't have the meaning the author wants. *Wounded* describes people who are hurt by other people—whether in a war or a violent attack. For example, you might come across *wounded* in sentences like these: "Two soldiers were wounded today..." or "A police officer was wounded when he was shot by a suspect..." To describe the people in this article, the author could use either *hurt* or *injured,* or vary the sentences by writing something like, "Dozens more ended up at local hospitals."
- The author uses important terms like *gusset plates* and *NTSB* without explaining them. Because of the other information in the paragraph, we can assume the intended audience is people who are not experts on this subject—people who need to have technical terms explained.
- The phrase *number of traffic* is incorrect. *Number of cars* or *amount of traffic* are much better alternatives; *In addition, an extra load of weight* is another phrase that needs revision. *In addition, there was extra weight* works better in the sentence.
- The author uses pronouns with unclear antecedents. In the final sentence, the author says, *this may be a growing problem,* but it's not clear what the word *this* refers to. Does *this* mean the extra weight, or the need for more construction on bridges?

Here is a revision of the paragraph. You should be able to see right away that it is significantly better:

> In August 2007, the I-35 bridge in Minneapolis, Minnesota, collapsed. Thirteen people were killed, and many others were injured in the tragedy. The National Transportation Safety Board (NTSB) investigated the accident and reported that the gusset plates, which fuse the metal structure together, were weak, and the bridge was not strong enough to support the amount of traffic that crossed it each day. Construction equipment added extra weight to the bridge and contributed to its fall. Since many of the state's bridges have not been renovated to support the increased number of cars on the road, similar disasters are likely to occur.

EXERCISE:

Here are two paragraphs on the same subject that have been submitted for the following U.S. history assignment: "Write a formal essay on some part of the federal government." Below are short *notes* the two writers took when investigating how the government deals with Presidential succession. These notes are accurate statements of the facts, just as a student might take them, complete with phrases, abbreviations, and poor punctuation. You need to make sure the writers presented them correctly:

- If Pres unable to continue b/c of death or impeachment, Veep takes over; 25th amend
- Pres can serve only two terms
- VP may serve more
- Only Constitutional duty of VP—breaking a tie vote in Senate
- VP and Pres before 1804 could be from different parties—potential problems; 12th amend
- VP was winner of next-to-largest number of votes

Which paragraph do you think best follows the samples, illustrations, and rules you have learned so far in the book and specifically in this chapter? Why did you make the choice you did? Provide specific examples to back up your choice.

Teacher's Note: We have constructed both paragraphs so that they contain problems that students should be able to recognize. There is no clear "better" paragraph. The issue, therefore, is for students to see, understand, and fix the errors in both essays; neither one is well written.

To extend this exercise, you might have students rewrite one of the paragraphs, eliminating and/or fixing the problems.

Paragraph A

If the President of the United States dies, is removed, or resigns, he or she is replaced by the Vice President, who is what the United States Constitution, designated in Amend 25, Paras 2 and 3, as the immediate successor to the President. The Veep, in fact, has no executive powers, but by voting, can break a tie vote in the Senate or the Congress. Although only two terms may be served by the President, anyone can be Vice President an infinite number of times. At one point in our grand history, the Vice President was only chosen by the democratic or republican party, not by the candidate of the winning election. The best part is that originally the Vice President was simply the person who gets the second-highest number of votes for President, so the President and Vice President were more or less opponents. That is, of course, if they were from opposite parties. Otherwise, they both could be from the same party and basically govern together as one.

Revisions will vary, as will reasons for the revisions. Possible areas for students to correct or rewrite:

If the President of the United States dies, is removed, or resigns, **(better logical order)** he or she is replaced by the Vice President, who is what the United States Constitution, designated in Amend 25, Paras 2 and 3, as the immediate successor to the President. **(awkward wording; unclear reference; abbreviations; repeated "United States")** The Veep **(slang)**, in fact **(filler words)** has no executive powers, but by voting, **(wordy)** can break a tie vote in the Senate or the Congress. **(factually incorrect according to student's own notes)** Although only two terms may be served by the President, **(passive voice not as strong as active)** anyone can be Vice President an infinite number of times.

(infinite is incorrect word; anyone is also incorrect; awkward wording) At one point in our grand **(grand is inappropriate for an objective essay)** history, the Vice President was only **(unnecessary and incorrect modifier)** chosen by the democratic or republican party **(passive voice; capitalization needed on Democratic, Republican, Party)**, not by the candidate of the winning election. **(wordy; incorrectly stated fact)** The best part **(slang; unnecessary; informal)** is that originally **(needs commas)** the Vice President was simply the person who gets **(informal; tense shift)** the second-highest number of votes for President, so the President and Vice President **(repetition is unnecessary)** were more or less opponents. **(filler words; tense issue in were)** That is, of course, if they were from opposite parties. **(unnecessary, already stated)** Otherwise, they both could be from the same party and basically govern together as one. **(Otherwise is too informal; basically is filler; "together as one" is unnecessary and redundant)**

Possible revision:

If the President of the United States dies, resigns, or is removed, he or she is replaced by the Vice President, who, according to the 25th amendment to the Constitution, is designated to succeed the President. The Vice President has no executive powers, but can break a tie vote in the Senate. Although the President may serve only two terms, there is no such limit on the Vice President. At one point in our history, the Democratic or Republican Party—not the winning candidate—chose the Vice President. One interesting fact is that, originally, the Vice President was the person who received the second-highest number of votes; theoretically, the President and Vice President could have been from opposing parties. That possibility no longer exists.

Paragraph B

If the President of the United States tragically dies before his term is up, resigns, or is removed from office by the discontented populace, the Vice President is granted the position. The VP does not have much executive authority, but he can brake a tie vote in the Senate, if ever there is one. The President can only serve two terms, a person can be VP times. In previous decades, the Vice President was chosen by his political affiliates instead of the presidential nominee. The VP was merely the runner-up in the election, and the President and Vice President were former adversaries forced to rule the country together.

Revisions will vary, as will reasons for the revisions. Possible areas for students to correct or rewrite:

If the President of the United States tragically **(filler word; emotions unnecessary in formal essay)** dies before his **(sexist language)** term is up **(illogical; if the person's term is over, he or she is no longer the President)**, resigns, or is removed from office by the discontented populace, **(factually incorrect according to notes; also suggests bias)** the Vice President is granted **(incorrect word usage; not factually correct in the notes; passive voice)** the position. The VP **(abbreviations are inappropriate in a formal essay)** may not have much executive authority **(vague word usage)**, but he can brake **(incorrect word)** a vote that is tied **(factually unclear)**, if ever there is one **(slang; filler words)**. The President can only serve two terms, **(only is misplaced; comma splice)** a person can be VP **(abbreviations are inappropriate in a formal paper)** times. **(missing word)** In previous decades, **(vague and non-specific words)** the Vice President was chosen by his political affiliates **(does not match the facts)** instead of the presidential nominee. **(incorrect modifier; sounds as if Vice President was chosen instead of the Presidential nominee)** The VP **(abbreviations are inappropriate in a formal paper)** was merely **(filler word)** the runner-up **(slang)** in the election, and the President and Vice President might be former adversaries **(incorrect tense)** forced to rule the country together. **(rule is wrong word)**

Possible revision:

If the President of the United States dies, resigns, or is removed from office, the Vice President takes over the position. The Vice President does not have any executive power, but he or she must break a tie vote in the Senate. One difference between the offices is that the President is limited to only two terms, but a person can serve as Vice President numerous times. Prior to 1804, the person who received the second-highest number of votes in the election automatically became Vice President. Therefore, the President and Vice President could have been former opponents who, together, would have had to govern the country.

Chapter Three

Incorporating Quotes

There are different ways to use **quotes** in your writing to make them more interesting other than using, "he said," or "she said," every time. Let's say you are writing about a recent study of brain tumors. As part of your investigation, you interview a research scientist, Brian Crop. Here is the exact transcript of one segment of the interview that you want to use in your essay:

> You: How fast do these tumors grow?
>
> Crop: Well, the tumors we are talking about at present are 'pineoblastomas,' fast-growing, but extremely rare types of brain tumors. They can double in size in a few weeks. Ten percent of the patients who develop this type of tumor will expire within six months, although scientific parameters have yet to be designed that can predict whether adults or children are most at risk, but evidence may be pointing to those below 21 as having the greatest propensity for developing the disease. Consequently, the only treatment for pineoblastomas is urgent and aggressive radiological or surgical treatment.

It should be clear to you that some words Crop used in his conversation are not important to the information you need to convey in your report—*Well, we are talking about at present*, and maybe *Consequently*. Other words and phrases such as, *expire, propensity*, and *scientific parameters have yet to be designed that can predict* may not be the exact language you want to use, either. You could work the necessary information, the material *you* want to use, into your report in a few ways:

One way is to actually use portions of what Crop said *within* your own sentence. For example:

> The study, according to researcher Brian Crop, followed "pineoblastomas," tumors that require "urgent and aggressive treatment." They "can double in size in a few weeks," and about ten percent of people with this type of tumor will die "within six months."

Note that there are only three facts Crop mentioned that you have included in this short paragraph:

1. the name and severity of the tumors
2. their tendency to grow quickly
3. the mortality rate of patients

A second technique is called **paraphrasing**. To *paraphrase* is to take an idea and put it into your own words. When you paraphrase, you still need to make sure of two things:

- Does your paraphrase *accurately* explain the ideas?
- Do you mention the person whose ideas you are using?

For a second paraphrase, which is based on the same interview, a different person, Alberto, might want to include only the following ideas:

1. the name of the tumor
2. the name of the doctor
3. the tumors' growth habits

Alberto does not want to write a long paraphrase, just a sentence. His paraphrase, therefore, might read something like this:

> Dr. Brian Crop studies pineoblastomas, which he claims are brain tumors that can double their size in a very short time.

Note that Alberto has not included *all* the information from the interview, just some of it, the information *he* considers important.

Make a list of at least three pieces of information that have been *left out* of Alberto's sentence.

> Answers will vary, but should include most of the following:
> - This type of brain tumor is rare.
> - Ten percent of patients will die within six months.
> - Scientists do not know who is most at risk.
> - Evidence shows that people under 21 may be more likely to get the tumor.
> - Treatment includes forceful, rapid radiology, and surgery.

Samantha, your classmate, has the exact same information as you and Alberto, but she wants to emphasize different things in her paper:

1. the patients' risk
2. treatment

Samantha's paraphrase will, therefore be quite different from the previous two:

Ten percent of patients who develop a certain type of brain tumor will die within a few months, but scientists cannot yet determine who is at greatest risk of developing this deadly brain disease. Treatment is limited to surgical removal or radiation therapy.

Make a list of at least three pieces of information that have been *left out* of Samantha's short paragraph. What one piece of information has she misstated slightly?

> Answers will vary, but should include the following:
> - The tumors are fast growing.
> - She also did not include the possibility that people under 21 may be more at risk.
> - There is no mention of "pineoblastomas," the name of the tumor.

> Samantha has altered a fact slightly. It would have been more accurate to write, "six months" than to use "a few months."

Cheryl, another classmate, wrote an *inaccurate* paraphrase from the same information. Look at hers, figure out what is wrong, and rewrite it.

Dr. Crop has explained that pineoblastomas will cause a patient's death within six months. He also claims that this specific type of tumor does not respond well to any treatments other than surgery and that children are most at risk.

Student revisions will vary, but should mention the three inaccuracies.

Dr. Crop has explained that pineoblastomas will cause a patient's death within six months. **(Only 10% will die within 6 months.)** He also claims that this specific type of tumor does not respond well to treatments other than surgery **(Radiation therapy also works.)** and that children are most at risk. **(Science has not yet arrived at an understanding of who is at risk.)**

Chapter Four

Using Transitions Effectively

What is a **transition**, and why is it important? Transitions are words or phrases that link parts of sentences, paragraphs, and essays to one another. They tell the reader the following:

Time Order	**Place**	**Effect**	**Contrast**
next	here	therefore	on the other hand
first	inside	so	but
afterwards	nearby	consequently	nevertheless
etc.	etc.	etc.	etc.

Summary	**Example**	**In Addition**
to conclude	for instance	also
briefly	specifically	and
finally	thus	too
etc.	etc.	besides
		etc.

There are many other examples of transitions, but they all serve the same purpose: Transitions lead your reader from one thought to another, from one sentence to another, or from one paragraph to the next. They join things that are separate and keep your writing flowing smoothly.

Earlier in this book, we talked about conjunctions, which are words like *and*, *so*, and *but*. These types of words link parts of a sentence. When you went over the correction of run-on sentences, you practiced showing the relationship between two clauses by using a conjunction or a semicolon.

Transitions are very much like conjunctions. They help the reader understand the relationship among ideas. Another benefit of using transitions is that they can prevent your sentences from being "jumpy," too short, and amateurish. Look at the following paragraph:

> The elderly Mrs. Kincaid put on her warmest hat. She put on a fur coat. It was freezing. She picked up her cane; she limped sadly toward the door. She opened it. Mrs. Kincaid's face gave her mood away. Her face was wet with tears. It was the day of her husband's funeral. She did not want to leave the house they had shared. She didn't even want to go to the funeral. She knew that she had to. Mr. Kincaid had been the most wonderful man she had ever known. He was dead. She remained alive. At the curb was a black car waiting to take her to the cemetery. She saw her grandkids. Her face managed a weak smile that grew larger. Mrs. Kincaid remembered all the reasons she had to be alive and happy.

You understand what is happening in this story, but something seems to be missing. All the ideas of the writer are equal and there is no flow to the paragraph. It jumps from one thing Mrs. Kincaid does to another with only a few connections. It needs a few more *transitions*. Now look at it again, after some transitions have been added:

> The elderly Mrs. Kincaid put on her warmest hat **and** a fur coat. It was freezing **outside**. She picked up her cane, limped sadly toward the door, **and** opened it. Mrs. Kincaid's face gave her mood away, **since** it was wet with tears. It was the day of her husband's funeral, **and** she did not want to leave the house they had shared **for more than fifty years**. She didn't even want to go to the funeral, **but, nevertheless,** she knew that she had to. **After all,** Mr. Kincaid had been the most wonderful man she had ever known, **but now** he was dead. She remained alive, **however**. **At the curb** was a black car waiting to take her to the cemetery, **and** she saw her grandkids **sitting in the backseat**. **Instantly,** her face managed a weak smile that grew larger **and** larger **as** she **now** remembered all the reasons she had to be alive and happy.

Identify all the transitions in these paragraphs by underlining them.

Paragraph A

First, I take everything off the counter. Then, I wipe down the counter with kitchen cleaner. Afterwards, I sort everything from the counter and the refrigerator. Finally, I take out the trash and recycling. At last, everything is done.

<u>First</u>, I take everything off the counter. <u>Then</u>, I wipe down the counter with kitchen cleaner. <u>Afterwards</u>, I sort everything from the counter <u>and</u> the refrigerator. <u>Finally</u>, I take out the trash <u>and</u> recycling. <u>At last</u>, everything is done.

Paragraph B

In addition to causing many students to take time away from studying, watching television is a barrier to good grades. First of all, students rush home to see the next episode of "All My Children" or reruns of "Millionaire." When test day comes, however, questions will not be on TV shows. Consequently, the students who waste their time in this way will usually have difficulties answering important questions. On the other hand, many of these students have better social lives than their friends who spend all their time studying. In conclusion, though, it's my opinion that TV should be restricted to weekends.

<u>In addition</u> to causing many students to take time away from studying, watching television is a barrier to good grades. <u>First of all</u>, students rush home to see the next episode of "All My Children" or reruns of "Millionaire." <u>When test day comes</u>, <u>however</u>, questions will not be on TV shows. <u>Consequently</u>, the students who waste their time in this way will usually have difficulties answering important questions. <u>On the other hand</u>, many of these students have better social lives than their friends who spend all their time studying. <u>In conclusion</u>, <u>though</u>, it's my opinion that TV should be restricted to weekends.

Paragraph C

Kashmir is a disputed territory between India and Pakistan. India thinks Kashmir belongs to it. However, Pakistan also claims the territory. Four Indo-Pakistani wars have been fought over the territory: in 1947, 1965, 1971, and 1999. Kashmir was then divided between India and Pakistan. Soon, Bangladesh, a part of India, declared independence. India and Pakistan began to develop nuclear weapons a few years later. The chances of war were lessened, but the costs of nuclear exchanges were far higher. Nowadays, India administers the territory in a way that makes human rights groups unhappy. Equally important, though, is that Pakistani soldiers are accused by India of committing violent acts within the region.

Kashmir is a disputed territory between India and Pakistan. India thinks Kashmir belongs to it. <u>However,</u> Pakistan <u>also</u> claims the territory. Four Indo-Pakistani wars have been fought over the territory: <u>in 1947, 1965, 1971, and 1999</u>. Kashmir was <u>then</u> divided between India and Pakistan. <u>Soon,</u> Bangladesh, a part of India, declared independence. India and Pakistan began to develop nuclear weapons <u>a few years later</u>. The chances of war were lessened, <u>but</u> the costs of nuclear exchanges were far higher. <u>Nowadays,</u> India administers the territory in a way that makes human rights groups unhappy. <u>Equally important, though,</u> is that Pakistani soldiers are accused by India of committing violent acts within the region.

One of the easiest and best ways to add transition and smoothness to your writing is to repeat important words or concepts, either by using the exact words or using pronouns to substitute for them. For example, in the following pairs of sentences, notice how the repeated parts help reinforce what the author wants to say:

Beans just taste terrible. Brown, white, kidney, wax—It doesn't matter. I hate beans!

In this sentence, *beans* is repeated only once, but the idea of disliking them is also repeated, reinforcing the author's feelings about them.

Beans just taste terrible. Brown beans, white beans, kidney beans, wax beans—it doesn't matter—I hate them!

In the second sentence, however, the emphasis is much stronger because of the continual restating of *beans*.

> Many people state that capital punishment is the best way to deter the crime of murder. Their argument is that a convicted murderer who is put to death can never kill again.

Note the use of similar phrases to convey the same message: *crime of murder, convicted murderer* and *capital punishment, put to death*.

> Many people argue that capital punishment is the best way to cut down on homicides because someone who is convicted of premeditated murder and is put to death cannot ever take another person's life.

In the second sentence, *homicides, premeditated murder* and *take another person's life* are all restatements of the same idea.

Your writing will improve by using transitions in all their forms. Do not use only one method. Sometimes, it's more helpful to use pronouns; sometimes, synonyms work better; sometimes, using a phrase to restate your important points is enough.

EXERCISE II:

Note how transitions are employed in the next paragraph. The repeated types of transitional elements are italicized, and the other transitions are underlined. Identify which word or phrase each of the *italicized transitional elements* stands for:

> Mr. Herman Palski, in 2004, invented a new method of removing unwanted "sludge" from car engines. <u>By 2008</u>, *he* was rich. The *invention* came about <u>because</u>, <u>one morning</u>, his car started to make noises at low speeds *that* went away when he reached *55 mph*. *Palksi* concluded that there were *excess deposits* in his *engine*, which were clogging *it* after the gasoline burned, <u>and</u> *these compounds* needed to be *eliminated*. <u>Because of this</u>, *Palski*, a retired scientist, *developed* "Unclog," a best-selling oil additive that helps concentrate the *deposits* so *they* can be *removed* during an oil change. <u>As a result</u>, *Palski's car* runs much better, and *he* has become a *multi-millionaire*. *His automobile problem*, <u>therefore</u>, has turned into a reward.

Transitional Element	**What it Stands For**
he	<u>Herman Palski</u>
invention	<u>a new method</u>
car	<u>car</u>
that	<u>noises</u>
55 mph	<u>speed</u>
Palksi	<u>Herman Palski</u>
excess deposits	<u>sludge</u>
engine	<u>engine</u>
it	<u>engine</u>
these compounds	<u>sludge</u>
eliminated	<u>removed</u>
Palski	<u>Herman Palski</u>
developed	<u>invented</u>
deposits	<u>sludge</u>
they	<u>sludge</u>
removed	<u>eliminated</u>
Palski's	<u>Herman Palski's</u>
car	<u>car</u>
he	<u>Herman Palski</u>
multi-millionaire	<u>rich</u>
His	<u>Herman Palski</u>
automobile	<u>car</u>
problem	<u>noises at low speeds that went away when he reached 55 mph</u>

Here is the same paragraph, *but* this time there are very few transitions. Notice the differences:

> Mr. Herman Palski, in 2004, invented a new method of removing unwanted "sludge" from car engines. By 2008, Palski was rich. The invention came about because, one morning, his car started to make noises at low speeds. The noises went away when he reached higher speeds. Palksi concluded that there was sludge in his car engine. The sludge was clogging the engine after the gasoline burned. The sludge needed to be removed from the engine. Palski, a retired scientist, invented "Unclog," a best-selling oil additive that helps concentrate the sludge so the sludge can be removed during an oil change. Palski's car runs much better. Palski has become rich. His car problem has turned into a reward.

You should immediately recognize that the first version is much smoother; the transitions help the ideas and sentences flow better. Using transitions effectively is necessary to make you a better writer, and you should make sure to include them to guide your reader from one thought to another.

Chapter Five

Emphasis and Subordination

When you write, it's important to place the parts of your paragraphs in a sensible order. If you allow the reader to be confused by the order, your writing will suffer. Writing should follow some sort of logical pattern. Some of your ideas are not as important as others. Consequently, the less important ones can be used to back up or support the more important ones. They can also supply examples. An idea that you want to highlight because you think it's important can be strategically placed within your paragraph. For instance, you could put it first. Or, you could lead up to it.

Let's look at the following paragraph:

There are several reasons for a child to learn to play an instrument. Studies have shown that students who are familiar with music do better in math. In addition, learning about music is a gateway to learning about all the other aspects of a culture: literature, art, history, etc. Music is also an excellent vehicle for developing social skills; students who learn to play in harmony with others respect their fellow human beings later in life. Many psychologists believe the same type of behavioral tendency also occurs in children who play sports. Both activities help socialization.

What is the most important sentence in that paragraph? Obviously, it is the first one. All the other sentences are less important; they are **subordinate** to the first, they support the first with reasons and examples, and they use facts to back up the information in the first. You probably already have learned that the most important sentence in a paragraph, the one that explains what the paragraph is *about*, is called the **topic sentence**. Topic sentences, however, can go anywhere in your paragraphs, and if you move these important sentences around, it helps supply variety to your writing.

Here is a new paragraph containing the same ideas as the previous one, but it has been slightly rewritten. The idea expressed in the topic sentence remains the same, but has been moved.

> Studies have shown that students who are familiar with music do better in math. In addition, learning about music is a gateway to learning about all the other aspects of a culture: literature, art, history, etc. Music is also an excellent vehicle for developing social skills; students who learn to play in harmony with others respect their fellow human beings later in life. Many psychologists believe the same type of behavioral tendency also occurs in children who play sports. Both activities help socialization. *These are just a few reasons for a child to learn to play an instrument.*

Here is yet another way to use a similar topic sentence; it's in the middle of the paragraph:

> Studies have shown that students who are familiar with music do better in math. In addition, learning about music is a gateway to learning about all the other aspects of a culture: literature, art, history, etc. *There are other reasons for a child to learn to play an instrument besides these two.* An additional reason is that music is an excellent vehicle for developing social skills; students who learn to play in harmony with others respect their fellow human beings later in life. Many psychologists believe the same type of behavioral tendency also occurs in children who play sports. Both activities help socialization.

When you write, try to make sure that your topic sentences are well constructed because they control the information in most paragraphs that you write.

EXERCISE:

The following paragraph is unfocused. There is no specific direction and no topic sentence to control what ideas the writer wants to stress. It wanders, almost as if the writer simply wrote the next thought that came into his or her mind.

Supply a good topic sentence for the paragraph and decide where your new sentence should go. You may also eliminate sentences that do not relate to your topic sentence, rearrange the order, or add a few sentences to support your new topic sentence.

In the fourteenth century, rats were responsible for causing millions of deaths throughout Europe. Rodents cause billions of dollars of damage to crops in today's society. There's an old saying that states, "Build a better mousetrap, and the world will beat a path to your door." Many traps nowadays will help keep the population of mice and rats down, but no one type is best in all situations. For example, the sticky traps mean that a person needs to throw away a mouse while it might still be alive. This method is also cruel because the animal may easily starve to death. Pivot traps and newer, scientific-types of mousetraps come into existence every year. Rats, mice, and other pests, however, are probably never going away.

Answers will vary. Possible revision:

There's an old saying that states, "Build a better mousetrap, and the world will beat a path to your door." Many traps nowadays will help keep the population of mice and rats down, but no one type is best in all situations. For example, the sticky traps mean that a person needs to throw away a mouse while it might still be alive. This method is also cruel because the animal may easily starve to death. A brand new type of trap involves a pivot point and a tunnel: When the animal enters the tunnel, its weight closes a door, and the person can simply throw the rat or mouse away and reset the trap. If you don't check it frequently, though, the rodent could starve there also. Some scientists have even developed a laser mousetrap. The problem with it is that it's much too expensive and takes a lot of equipment to set up. Based on experience, rats, mice, and other pests, however, are probably never going away.

Cumulative Exercises

These exercises offer you the opportunity to put what you
have learned throughout *Maximum Impact* to work.

Correct the run-on sentences, the comma splices, and the fragments. Some tenses of verbs and verb forms will need fixing. There are also mistakes in end punctuation and subject-verb agreement. You will need to rewrite some sentences to make them correct. Once again, there is no one perfect way to fix many of these mistakes. Various possibilities do exist.

Teacher's Note: We have not supplied all of the possible revisions, as there are many variations. In addition, the method of turning fragments into sentences will vary from one student to the next.

1. After Billy and his brother go to the zoo, their father took them back home.

   After Billy and his brother went to the zoo, their father took them back home.

   OR

   After Billy and his brother go to the zoo, their father takes them back home.

   OR

   After Billy and his brother go to the zoo, their father will take them back home.

2. Until last season, my high school football team had won only three games in four years, we win six in 2002, however.

   Until last season, my high school football team had won only three games in four years. We won six in 2002, however.

   OR

   Until last season, my high school football team had won only three games in four years. However, we won six in 2002.

3. How are the fish you bought last week my brother says that you purchased some beauties.

    How are the fish you bought last week? My brother says that you purchased some beauties.

4. Only one of the computers are still working since the power failure.

    Only one of the computers is still working since the power failure.

5. Why that baby cries all the time?

    Why does that baby cry all the time?

6. Alfredo Benitez made a tremendously important discovery, he diagrams how sunlight affect sea creatures in the deepest parts of the ocean.

    Alfredo Benitez made a tremendously important discovery; he diagrammed how sunlight affects sea creatures in the deepest parts of the ocean.

7. Nobody in the neighbors' houses pay attention to the traffic.

    Nobody in the neighbors' houses pays attention to the traffic.

8. First, Jimmy ate all his supper then he finishes his dessert.

    First, Jimmy ate all his supper, and, then he finished his dessert.

    OR

    First, Jimmy ate all his supper; then, he finished his dessert.

9. How are you feeling Karen said you were sick.

    How are you feeling? Karen said you were sick.

10. My classroom has twenty-eight chairs in it, aren't there are thirty kids, though.

    My classroom has twenty-eight chairs in it. Aren't there thirty kids, though?

    OR

    My classroom has twenty-eight chairs in it, but there are thirty kids.

11. We will do this first then we decided what to do next.

    We will do this first. Then, we'll decide what to do next.

    OR

    We did this first, and, then, we decided what to do next.

12. That hurts my thumb, stop.

    That hurts my thumb! Stop!

13. Because I said so!

    Do it because I said so!

14. Apples are available in many different types, some are sweet, some are tart, and some had a comination of flavors.

    Apples are available in many different types. Some are sweet, some are tart, and some have a combination of flavors.

15. If you want to win the championship, all it took was practice, desire, and some luck.

    If you want to win the championship, all it takes is practice, desire, and some luck.

16. Even though there were enough food for everyone at the party.

    Even though there was enough food for everyone at the party, some guests still complained.

17. Is the cake ready yet. I'll be hungry.

    Is the cake ready yet? I'm hungry.

18. How hard did you have to study to get an A on that test.

    How hard did you have to study to get an A on that test?

19. Whoever caught the biggest fish.

    Whoever caught the biggest fish won a thousand dollars.

20. The air in the office caused my skin to turn dry, I am using lotion every day.

    The air in the office caused my skin to turn dry, so I am using lotion every day.

    OR

    The air in the office caused my skin to turn dry, even though I had used lotion every day.

Use commas and semicolons to punctuate the items in series correctly. For this exercise, all punctuation marks that you see in the sentences are used properly, so you should leave these as they are.

1.　The best ways to learn to play a musical instrument are by following a teacher's instructions by reading sheet music or by imitating sounds on a CD.

   The best ways to learn to play a musical instrument are by following a teacher's instructions, by reading sheet music, or by imitating sounds on a CD.

2.　The refrigerator was broken the ice cream was defrosted and the steaks were ruined.

   The refrigerator was broken, the ice cream was defrosted, and the steaks were ruined.

3.　We ate the salad, which was a little too cold the main course, consisting of steak lobster and mashed potatoes, which was delicious and the dessert, which tasted absolutely amazing.

   We ate the salad, which was a little too cold; the main course, consisting of steak, lobster, and mashed potatoes, which was delicious; and the dessert, which tasted absolutely amazing.

4.　Oregon Kansas Hawaii Alaska and Nevada are the only states that have only six letters in their names.

   Oregon, Kansas, Hawaii, Alaska, and Nevada are the only states that have only six letters in their names.

5. My favorite snacks include potato chips peanut butter and jelly and ice cream.

   My favorite snacks include potato chips, peanut butter and jelly, and ice cream.

6. The dust came into the cabin through the cracks in the windowpane through a small hole by the door through an opening near the ceiling and through the badly made roof.

   The dust came into the cabin through the cracks in the windowpane, through a small hole by the door, through an opening near the ceiling, and through the badly made roof.

7. Many large tan and hungry lions surrounded the buffalo.

   Many large, tan, and hungry lions surrounded the buffalo.

8. The long thick dark-colored streak of mineral deep inside the mine turned out to be a huge deposit of cobalt, which is a mineral necessary to manufacture some medicines batteries for hybrid cars steel ceramics and even some brands of makeup.

   The long, thick, dark-colored streak of mineral deep inside the mine turned out to be a huge deposit of cobalt, which is a mineral necessary to manufacture some medicines, batteries for hybrid cars, steel, ceramics, and even some brands of makeup.

9. Dictionaries an encyclopedia magazine articles and even a set of speeches were thrown across my desk so I could do my research without getting up.

Dictionaries, an encyclopedia, magazine articles, and even a set of speeches were thrown across my desk so I could do my research without getting up.

10. The new President's economic policies include a tax plan to assist lower-income families, whose wages have dropped in the past four years two months of reduced taxes on purchases over $10,000, supposedly designed to stimulate spending increases in government-sponsored jobs, which are expected to stimulate job growth and the appointment of Henry Patrick Samuelson, a Nobel Prize-winning economist, to the President's Cabinet.

The new President's economic policies include a tax plan to assist lower-income families, whose wages have dropped in the past four years; two months of reduced taxes on purchases over $10,000, supposedly designed to stimulate spending; increases in government-sponsored jobs, which are expected to stimulate job growth; and the appointment of Henry Patrick Samuelson, a Nobel Prize-winning economist, to the President's Cabinet.

Rewrite these sentences that have errors in modifiers and apostrophes. For this exercise, all punctuation marks that you see in the sentences are used properly, so you should leave these as they are.

Teacher's Note: We have supplied at least one alternative possibility to correct these sentences.

1. My brothers thoroughbred horse, which he only rides on weekends, broke out of it's stable and ran away.

    My brother's thoroughbred horse, which he rides only on weekends, broke out of its stable and ran away.

    OR

    My brother's thoroughbred horse, which he rides on weekends only, broke out of its stable and ran away.

2. Walking down the hall, the old grandfathers clock struck midnight, and all the visitors woke up.

    When we were walking down the hall, the old grandfather's clock struck midnight, and all the visitors woke up.

    OR

    Walking down the hall, we heard the old grandfather's clock strike midnight, and all the visitors woke up.

3. Please don't touch that airplane model before being completely assembled.

    Please don't touch that airplane model before it's completely assembled.

    OR

    Please don't touch that airplane model until it is completely assembled.

4. Floating in the Mississippi River, the water feel's cold.

Whenever we float in the Mississippi River, the water feels cold.

OR

Floating in the Mississippi River, we felt cold.

5. Stranded on a desert island, the sun blazed down intensely.

Stan was stranded on a desert island, and the sun blazed down intensely.

OR

Stranded on a desert island, Stan felt the sun blazing down intensely.

OR

The sun blazed down intensely on Stan, who was stranded on a desert island.

6. In order to become a great conductor, all members of the orchestra must appreciate you're ability's.

In order to become a great conductor, you must make certain that all members of the orchestra appreciate your abilities.

OR

For you to become a great conductor, you must make certain that all members of the orchestra appreciate your abilities.

OR

You must make certain that all members of the orchestra appreciate your abilities before you can become a great conductor.

7. After putting the saddles on, the horses's bridles and reins were adjusted.

    After the jockeys put saddles on the horses, the bridles and reins were adjusted.

    OR

    After the horses' saddles were put on, the bridles and reins were adjusted.

    OR

    After we put saddles on the horses, we adjusted the bridles and reins.

8. While waiting for the electricians helper to return with tools, the TV stopped working.

    The TV stopped working while we were waiting for the electrician's helper to return with tools.

    OR

    While we waited for the electrician's helper to return with tools, the TV stopped working.

9. Poisonous fish live in all areas of the ocean, which can cause any careless swimmers death.

    Poisonous fish, which can cause the death of any careless swimmer, live in all areas of the ocean.

    OR

    Poisonous fish, which can cause any careless swimmer's death, live in all areas of the ocean.

10. Watching Shakespeares *Hamlet*, the frightening appearance of Hamlets dead father, certainly surprised us.

    Watching Shakespeare's *Hamlet*, we were certainly surprised by the frightening appearance of Hamlet's dead father.

    OR

    When we were watching Shakespeare's Hamlet, the frightening appearance of Hamlet's dead father certainly surprised us.

Correct the apostrophe use in the following sentences. Some sentences contain more than one apostrophe error.

1. Both Elizabeth and Tony's houses will be empty tomorrow.

   Both Elizabeth's and Tony's houses will be empty tomorrow.

2. The pages' were ripped, and the books covers were torn off.

   The pages were ripped, and the books' covers were torn off.

3. None of the boys math score's was high enough to qualify for the BrainStrain competition.

   None of the boys' math scores was high enough to qualify for the BrainStrain competition.

4. The five scientist's new discoveries centered on three female foxes dens and they're cubs eating habits.

   The five scientists' new discoveries centered on three female foxes' dens and their cubs' eating habits.

5. The only things the store sells that are suitable for peoples' Halloween needs would be three witch's costumes or a jesters hat and shoes.

   The only things the store sells that are suitable for people's Halloween needs would be three witches' costumes or a jester's hat and shoes.

6. The womens soccer field is right here, but the man's soccer field is around the corner.

   The women's soccer field is right here, but the men's soccer field is around the corner.

7. Shell be home in ten minute's.

    She'll be home in ten minutes.

8. How many As did you get on last months report card?

    How many A's did you get on last month's report card?

9. Billy Jones girlfriends' car need's new brake's because she wore the original one's out.

    Billy Jones's girlfriend's car needs new brakes because she wore the original ones out.

10. Only one of James friend's owns a car.

    Only one of James's friends owns a car.

11. Young childrens accomplishments's in elementary school generally start with making cursive letter's correctly.

    Young children's accomplishments in elementary school generally start with making cursive letters correctly.

12. The girls sports teams did much better than the boys teams did in every one of the last five years championship games.

    The girls' sports teams did much better than the boys' teams did in every one of the last five years' championship games.

13. Doesnt it seem cute that the babies hat is the wrong size?

    Doesn't it seem cute that the baby's hat is the wrong size?

14. Her sister-in-laws visit lasted only one day.

    Her sister-in-law's visit lasted only one day.

15. John Hughes Diner is closed Wednesdays, but its very popular the rest of the week.

    John Hughes's Diner is closed Wednesdays, but it's very popular the rest of the week.

16. Carole's and Sara's trip to Washington included a stop at the Vietnam Veteran's Wall, where the names, of soldier's are inscribed.

    Carole and Sara's trip to Washington included a stop at the Vietnam Veterans' Wall, where the names of soldiers are inscribed.

17. We saved fifteen dollars worth of coupons and took them to the store.

    We saved fifteen dollars' worth of coupons and took them to the store.

18. Both glasses designs had been hand-painted.

    Both glasses' designs had been hand-painted.

19. The doctors patients all respected her because of her skill's.

    The doctor's patients all respected her because of her skills.

20. Jerry's brothers cars include a rare, 1935 Rolls Royce.

    Jerry's brother's cars include a rare, 1935 Rolls Royce.

    OR

    Jerry's brothers' cars include a rare, 1935 Rolls Royce.

Correct all the subject-verb agreement errors in the following sentences:

1. Only one of the boys were competing for a trophy.

    Only one of the boys was competing for a trophy.

2. All sections of the fence is complete now.

    All sections of the fence are complete now.

3. Both the monitors and the computer was stored in a cool room.

    Both the monitors and the computer were stored in a cool room.

4. Around us in every direction was fans of the other team.

    Around us in every direction were fans of the other team.

5. In each cubicle where I work, there is a filing cabinet, bookshelves, and a computer.

    In each cubicle where I work, there are a filing cabinet, bookshelves, and a computer.

6. A bread and butter sandwich go on the plate with eggs today.

    A bread and butter sandwich goes on the plate with eggs today.

7. Neither Bette nor her sisters likes football.

    Neither Bette nor her sisters like football.

8. Either Gloria, Carmen, or Juanita are being honored at tonight's awards ceremony.

    Either Gloria, Carmen, or Juanita is being honored at tonight's awards ceremony.

9. Measles are a bad disease in young children.

    Measles is a bad disease in young children.

10. The teacher, as well as her assistants, know how to explain scientific facts.

    The teacher, as well as her assistants, knows how to explain scientific facts.

In the following sentences, fix any pronouns that are used incorrectly. Some sentences are correct as written.

1. Joanie and me will go to that party.

    Joanie and I will go to that party.

2. Dad asked if Terrance and her had left the door unlocked.

    Dad asked if Terrance and she had left the door unlocked.

3. She and him both had overdue library books.

    She and he both had overdue library books.

4. Me and her had gone to the party last night.

    She and I had gone to the party last night.

5. That birthday present is for him, not she.

    That birthday present is for him, not her.

6. He aimed the dodge ball at us.

    Correct

7. Because the cats were so loud, the neighbors threw sticks at they.

    Because the cats were so loud, the neighbors threw sticks at them.

8. Norman and me were best friends a long time ago.

    Norman and I were best friends a long time ago.

9. The problem was too difficult for she.

    The problem was too difficult for her.

10. It was him who forgot the tickets.

    It was he who forgot the tickets.

Place quotation marks, and any other marks of punctuation that are needed for your corrections, in the sentences that need them. A few sentences will need single and double quotation marks. Only one sentence is correct as written. All punctuation marks that you see in the sentences are used properly, so you should leave them as they are.

1. Why is that little kid dressed up we asked.

    "Why is that little kid dressed up?" we asked.

2. The teacher asked if anyone had read Poe's famous poem, The Raven.

    The teacher asked if anyone had read Poe's famous poem, "The Raven."

3. After the accident, the driver who was at fault said he was sorry.

    Correct

4. If this is the way you see it, Mr. Henderson said, we need to discuss it much further.

    "If this is the way you see it," Mr. Henderson said, "we need to discuss it much further."

5. The man in the audience asked the speaker Who was the first explorer to locate the source of the Nile River

    The man in the audience asked the speaker, "Who was the first explorer to locate the source of the Nile River?"

6. Laura said, My professor announced in class, There will be a short quiz on George Washington, but I wasn't listening.

    Laura said, "My professor announced in class, 'There will be a short quiz on George Washington,' but I wasn't listening."

7.   The prisoner thought, If only I had not been in the gang, I wouldn't be stuck in jail!

The prisoner thought, "If only I had not been in the gang, I wouldn't be stuck in jail!"

8.   When did the star of the movie ask Who is willing to risk everything for love

When did the star of the movie ask, "Who is willing to risk everything for love"?

9.   The words, I'm sorry for everything I did before I knew you don't mean much right now said Helene through her tears.

"The words, 'I'm sorry for everything I did before I knew you' don't mean much right now," said Helene through her tears.

10. Didn't your mom say You're grounded! at least twice last week

Didn't your mom say, "You're grounded!" at least twice last week?

11. Anyone said the speaker, who purchases a car from that dealership is sure to pay too much.

"Anyone," said the speaker, "who purchases a car from that dealership is sure to pay too much."

12. The villain in that story shouted You'll never take me alive! and he was right.

The villain in that story shouted, "You'll never take me alive!" and he was right.

13. He told the doctor, My father always said Eat your eggs raw, and you'll stay healthy, but I never listened to him.

    He told the doctor, "My father always said, 'Eat your eggs raw, and you'll stay healthy,' but I never listened to him."

14. The reporter announced, The race for Governor has been decided, and the loser has declared, We must all now support Governor Casey.

    The reporter announced, "The race for Governor has been decided, and the loser has declared, 'We must all now support Governor Casey.' "

15. The quotation that includes the words, When in the course of human events begins The Declaration of Independence.

    The quotation that includes the words, "When in the course of human events" begins the Declaration of Independence.

Insert all necessary commas in the sentences. Some sentences are correct as written and will not need any commas.

1. First let's get our clothes ready.

    First, let's get our clothes ready.

2. All students who get straight A's will be allowed to go on the field trip.

    Correct

3. On April 14 2008 we visited the house of England's Prime Minister.

    On April 14, 2008, we visited the house of England's Prime Minister.

4. Edgar Allan Poe was born on January 19 1908 in Boston Massachusetts and he suffered many hardships during his first five years of life.

    Edgar Allan Poe was born on January 19, 1908, in Boston, Massachusetts, and he suffered many hardships during his first five years of life.

5. I really like bananas but ate too many once and I was sick for a few days.

    I really like bananas, but ate too many once, and I was sick for a few days.

6. Santa Claus who is based upon a Dutch legend about a man living in the far North Country now occupies a place in our country's heritage, thanks to the first cartoon of him which showed a fat, elf-like figure holding toys.

    Santa Claus, who is based upon a Dutch legend about a man living in the far North Country, now occupies a place in our country's heritage, thanks to the first cartoon of him, which showed a fat, elf-like figure holding toys.

7. Shortly after Jeremy left the movie.

    Shortly after, Jeremy left the movie.

8. The author who has just completed her second book will speak at the library.

    The author, who has just completed her second book, will speak at the library.

9. Concerns rose for the stranded hikers but not until the weather turned bitterly cold.

    Concerns rose for the stranded hikers, but not until the weather turned bitterly cold.

10. Prior to that store's opening we had to go across town for prescriptions.

    Prior to that store's opening, we had to go across town for prescriptions.

11. Both cars that you drive have problems with their brakes which need to be repaired immediately.

    Both cars that you drive have problems with their brakes, which need to be repaired immediately.

12. Statements about his musical abilities which had been made since his second birthday were highly exaggerated.

    Statements about his musical abilities, which had been made since his second birthday, were highly exaggerated.

13. The score was 57 to 54 not 57 to 44.

    The score was 57 to 54, not 57 to 44.

14. Any parents who drive their children to our off-campus school which is located two miles north of our main campus need to arrive at least an hour early.

    Any parents who drive their children to our off-campus school, which is located two miles north of our main campus, need to arrive at least an hour early.

15. The news that I watched on television last night depressed me.

    Correct

16. Scientists who work on nutritional aspects of food declared today that eggs are not a serious contributor to high cholesterol.

    Correct

17. Outside the door kept banging against the side of the barn.

    Outside, the door kept banging against the side of the barn.

18. The principal praised the students who have been accepted to college early.

    Correct

19. The boxer finally retired but not until he suffered a severe concussion in his last bout which ended his career.

    The boxer finally retired, but not until he suffered a severe concussion in his last bout, which ended his career.

20. In my opinion the President who won last year's election is doing a great job.

    In my opinion, the President who won last year's election is doing a great job.

For each sentence, circle the correct word(s) from the pairs in parentheses.

1. No one could make the ropes (**loose,** lose) enough.

2. What's the (**weather,** whether) like?

3. One major (**principle,** principal) that I'll never give up is that people are basically good.

4. Don't (**alter,** altar) your plans just because of me.

5. I'm not sure what (affect, **effect**) that storm will have on traffic.

6. The (**angles,** angels) we measured were all equal.

7. No one walked (passed, **past**) the display without stopping.

8. (Their, **They're,** There) the people we want to follow.

9. Get your clothes (**all ready,** already) for the party.

10. What (**advice,** advise) would you give me?

11. The mysterious (**illusion,** allusion) performed by the magician was fascinating.

12. Wow! That material is very (course, **coarse**).

13. The (capitol, **capital**) of my country is Lima.

14. Rain really (effects, **affects**) people's behavior, especially when (they're, **their,** there) plans have to change.

15. (Its, **It's**) time to turn (you're, **your**) television off, (to, **too,** two).

16. John couldn't decide (weather, **whether**) or not he should (<u>except,</u> **accept**) the package.

17. In order (<u>too, two,</u> **to**) fix what is wrong, (**your,** you're) first step should be (<u>too, two,</u> **to**) (**lose,** loose) the incorrect ideas you held in the (**past,** passed).

18. (Accept, **Except**) for the empty (Capital, **Capitol**) Building, Washington was very crowded.

19. I found (**your,** you're) favorite movie on the Internet. Now, (<u>your,</u> **you're**) able to see it for free.

20. (<u>They're, Their,</u> **There**) will be at least (<u>too,</u> **two,** to) other chances for me to (**advise,** advice) you on important matters.

21. The movie lost (<u>it's,</u> **its**) top spot after (<u>it's,</u> **its**) short time as the number one film in the country.

22. The team's players were (**already,** all ready) on the bus, and they were (<u>already,</u> **all ready**) to go.

23. My term paper did not mention the (**allusion,** illusion) to Shakespeare.

24. To determine the (<u>affects,</u> **effects**) of tobacco use, scientists conducted an experiment.

25. The priest stood at the (<u>alter,</u> **altar**) writing; then he (**passed,** past) his sermon to his secretary.

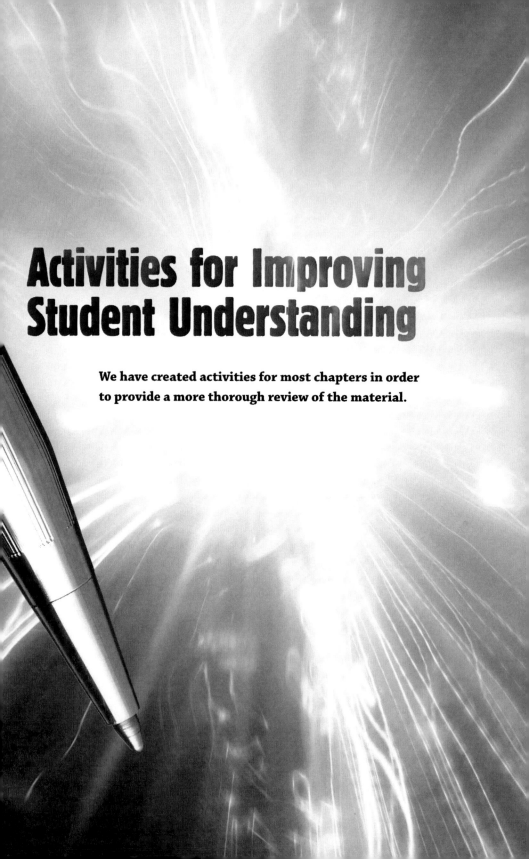

Activities for Improving Student Understanding

We have created activities for most chapters in order to provide a more thorough review of the material.

Part I: Sentence Sense

Chapter One: What makes a complete sentence?

A)   Read the following dependent clauses to the class and have students volunteer answers that will complete the sentences:

1.   Whenever I see that movie

2.   Because my motorcycle is in the shop

3.   Until I got a dog

4.   Since they never collect the garbage

5.   Wherever Peggy goes

Answers will vary.

B)   Pick five students. Give each student a card or large sheet of paper with one of the following dependent clauses on it:

1.   Until she saw the color of the paint,

2.   When I heard the loud sirens,

3.   Although Kaley wanted to know the answer,

4.   Because Andrew admitted he wrote the note,

5.   While Raj's house was being renovated,

Give five other students a card that has one of the following independent clauses on it:

a.   Joanne wasn't sure whether she was going to like the new room.

b.   no one told her.

c.   Rosa is not going to stay angry with him.

d.   he lived with a relative.

e.   I hoped that the fire trucks were not going to my house again.

Have students with the second set of cards stand next to the correct beginning of their sentence so that, when placed together, they make a complete thought.

Answers:
1.   a
2.   e
3.   b
4.   c
5.   d

C)   Ask students to write a five-sentence paragraph about any topic. Because they will be read by other students in the class, the paragraphs do not need to be factual; in fact, the more made-up information in them, the better, as that will preserve the writer's anonymity.

The students should not put their names on the paragraphs. When they are finished, collect all the paragraphs, mix them up, assign a code letter or number to each one to identify them later, and pass them out at random. Each student will work on his or her anonymous paragraph throughout this first section, making changes that improve the original. This will help them look at writing with fresh eyes.

After enough time for each type of correction has elapsed, collect the papers and redistribute them to their original owners. The writers would then be able to see the issues the proofreader has found.

Answers will vary.

A)   Divide the students into groups of four or five. Each group will write a dialogue for two people on a topic of its choosing. The dialogues should be very brief—one sentence per person, with each person speaking no more than three or four times. The groups will then speak their dialogues aloud while the other groups try to transcribe the sentences using correct capitalization and end punctuation. Students should not worry about internal punctuation until later. This activity can be repeated at any time to stress the concept under consideration.

Answers will vary.

B)   Have students read the following examples aloud and explain why each one is or is not a complete sentence:

1.   Very few people know the true meaning of success.

2.   Beyond the wall.

3.   Was a result of the disease.

4.   When you grow up in a big family, you're always looking for attention.

5.   One person.

6.   If the ship comes in.

7.   Are you ready?

8.   Whenever I wonder?

9.   The Egyptians and Cleopatra.

10. Sometimes, nothing works correctly.

One way to approach this activity is to write each fragment on the board, use transparancies or a Powerpoint presentation and have one student at a time complete the fragment. Another possibility would be to have students submit ideas, and the class could vote on which correction it likes the best. If students are encountering difficulties, the questions that follow the fragments can be used to stimulate answers.

1.   Fatimah, my sister.

     What is Fatimah doing? Is it possible that something was done to her?

2.   The pencil and the notebook.

     Did someone use the pencil and the notebook? Did they fall off a desk?

3.   Looked around the room before slowly walking away.

     Who or what looked around the room?

4.   Because Jonathon caused the accident.

     What happened because of the accident?

5.   Never saw that movie before.

     Who never saw that movie before?

6.   In the kitchen?

     What is/was happening in the kitchen? Who is/was involved?

7.   When you tell José that.

     What will be the result of telling José?

8.   To climb the highest mountain in Alaska and do it without any guides.

     Does someone want to climb this mountain?

9.   Running as fast as he could and finally reaching the finish line in first place.

     What happened after he won?

10. Although women can withstand more pain than men can.

     What does this fact lead to?

Part II: Avoiding Ambiguity

Chapter One: Modifiers

Incorrect use of modifiers can provide a great deal of interesting fun for students who can make them up. It is also enjoyable for classes to explain their meanings as written, since the sentence frequently indicates something that is impossible or silly.

You can divide the class into two teams and go through the following activity by having students decipher the actual meanings of the sentences and then having them come up with one or two corrected sentences.

1. The store helps customers select the right tool with no previous knowledge.

2. When we were at the aquarium, I found a fish for my brother I called Nemo.

3. Swimming through the water, dry land was all the man overboard craved.

4. Crawling through the open bedroom window, I saw the burglar.

5. The old man, a writer, said that he writes for six hours a day on television.

6. Toby noticed a car in the driveway that was painted white and black yesterday.

7. Everyone knew on Friday there would be a party at my house.

8. To be elected President, money cannot be underestimated.

9. Having just had a huge snack, a cheeseburger just didn't appeal to Robbie.

10. Opening at midnight, I made my way to the Bowling League's first night.

11. I only hate my dog when she wakes me up to go out late at night.

12. Chewing rapidly and swallowing just as fast, the food tasted delicious.

13. Arguing for over an hour, the dispute was finally solved.

14. To get a passport, two forms of identification are necessary.

15. Gabriel saw a young man walking down the street in his suit.

16. I bought a new DVD at the computer store that was broken in three places.

17. The clown entertained the child who was making balloon animals.

18. Important information will be available upon leaving the area.

19. With the right information, a good research paper can earn an A+.

20. Being relaxed, the interview with the President was smooth and free of confrontation.

Part III: Show You Know

Chapter Two: Apostrophes

Using Apostrophes to show possession

Some of these sentences can be illustrated on the board (1, 2, 4, 5, 8, and 9). Choose students to be the artists for these six sentences; the other sentences can be discussed without a drawing. Read the sentence aloud and have the student draw a picture of it, as he or she understands it, which is the important part. Write the sentence, uncorrected, under the picture. Then, ask the questions that are provided. Continue through the activity in the same manner.

A)   Carlise thought she saw a crack in the <u>eggs</u> shell.

    1.   Is there one egg or more than one egg?

    One

    2.   How can you tell?

    The word *shell* is singular; there would be more than one shell for more than one egg.

    3.   Put the apostrophe where it should go in this sentence.

    Carlise thought she saw a crack in the egg's shell.

    4.   Write a similar sentence and change the number of the underlined word.

    Carlise thought she saw cracks in the eggs' shells.

B) The <u>students</u> desks were all pushed together so that they could talk to each other.

1. Do the desks belong to one student or more than one student?

More than one

2. How can you tell?

The first clue is the word *desks*. If there are multiple desks, there are probably multiple students. Then, we have *they* and *each other*, making it clear that there are multiple students.

3. Put the apostrophe where it should go in this sentence.

The students' desks were all pushed together so that they could talk to each other.

4. Write a similar sentence and change the number of the underlined word.

The student's desk was pushed against the wall.

C) <u>Ambers</u> friend Marc got her tickets to the music festival, so she took a day off work.

1. Is there more than one Amber, or only one?

One

2. How can you tell?

Amber is the first name of a person. If it were the last name of a family, it would have a word like *the* attached to it (The Ambers had a picnic for their neighbors.) In addition, the words *her* and *she* are singular.

3. Put the apostrophe where it should go in this sentence.

Amber's friend Marc got her tickets to the music festival, so she took a day off work.

4. Is there a way to change the number the underlined word?

No

D)   The <u>houses</u> roof was damaged, and the windows were broken.

1.   Is there one house or more than one house?

One

2.   How can you tell?

There is only one *roof*. If there were multiple houses, the sentence would say roofs, and the verb would be *were*.

3.   Put the apostrophe where it should go in this sentence.

The houses roof was damaged, and the windows were broken.

4.   Write a similar sentence and change the number of the underlined word.

The houses' roofs were damaged, and the windows were broken.

E)   Officer Rosario left flyers with pictures of the missing man on all the <u>cars</u> windshields.

1.   Is there more than one car, or one?

More than one

2.   How can you tell?

The word *windshields* is plural; the word *all* is also a clue.

3.   Where should the apostrophe go?

After the s

4.   Write a similar sentence and change the number of the underlined word.

Officer Rosario left flyers with pictures of the missing man on a car's windshield.

F) Because of the economy, all <u>workers</u> hours were cut in half.

   1. Whose hours were cut?

   The workers had their hours cut.

   2. Is the underlined word singular or plural, and how can you tell?

   The word is plural. It would be incorrect to think that there was only one worker, especially since the word *all* is modifying workers.

   3. Where should the apostrophe go? Explain your answer.

   It should go after the final s on *workers*. The *hours* belong to both the workers, so the plural needs the apostrophe.

   4. Write a sentence with a similar idea that uses two apostrophes.

   Because of the economy, all workers' hours were cut in half, but the supervisors' hours were not.

G) <u>Beth</u> and <u>Al</u> divorce is finally complete, but they want to remain friends.

   1. Whose divorce is it?

   It belongs to both people.

   2. Where should the *apostrophes* go?

   It should go after *Al*.

   3. Write a similar sentence that uses two apostrophes.

   Beth Mikkel's and Al Grand's divorces were completed on the same day.

H) The teacher misplaced <u>everybodys</u> books.

    1.   Is the word *everybodys* singular or plural?

    It means each and every student, so it is singular.

    2.   Where should you put an apostrophe?

    It should go before the s.

    3.   Write a similar sentence that uses no apostrophes.

    The teacher misplaced their books.

I) My <u>mother-in-laws</u> favorite hobby is bowling, so I bought her bowling shoes.

    1.   Is the underlined word singular or plural? Explain your answer.

    It must be singular, based on the rest of the sentence and because a person can have only one mother-in-law at a time.

    2.   Place the apostrophe in the proper location.

    mother-in-law's

    3.   Rewrite the sentence so there is no apostrophe.

    The favorite hobby of my mother-in-law is bowling.

J) The <u>Yankees</u> and the <u>Dodgers</u> mascots both showed up to practice at the same time.

    1.   What words need to take apostrophes?

    Yankees and Dodgers

    2.   Where would the apostrophes go? Explain your reasoning.

    Yankees' and Dodgers'. The teams are separate from each other, both teams are plural, and both end in s.

    3.   Write a similar sentence that uses no apostrophes in the nouns.

    The mascot for the Yankees and the mascot for the Dodgers showed up to practice at the same time.

Using Apostrophes to Form Contractions

For this activity, read the following sentences aloud. Each student will write down the sentence the way he or she thinks it should be written, changing words to form contractions.

1. He will not be going to the party.

   He won't be going to the party.

2. Why are you not glad to see me?

   Why aren't you glad to see me?

3. Hal has not arrived yet.

   Hal hasn't arrived yet.

4. Conrad does not know where the package is.

   Conrad doesn't know where the package is.

5. Do not do that, or you will pay the consequences. (two contractions)

   Don't do that, or you'll pay the consequences.

6. That cannot be the right answer because it is not possible. (two contractions)

   That can't be the right answer because it's not possible.

   OR

   That can't be the right answer because it isn't possible.

7. Why will you not take out the garbage?

   Why won't you take out the garbage?

8. Unless you will be late, do not call. (two contractions)

   Unless you'll be late, don't call.

9. Either you have not studied, or you must have forgotten it all. (two contractions)

   Either you haven't studied, or you must've forgotten it all.

10. You are the best singer in the group.

    You're the best singer in the group.

11. Darlene is going.

    Darlene's going.

12. We did not know who is going to be watching the store. (two contractions)

    We didn't know who's going to be watching the store.

13. Why can Sheila's dad not see what a great person she is? (only one contraction)

    Why can't Sheila's dad see what a great person she is?

14. Everybody is standing for the last minute of the game.

    Everybody's standing for the last minute of the game.

15. Kyle and his brothers have not gone this way before.

    Kyle and his brothers haven't gone this way before.

The Difference Between *Its* and *It's*

For this short activity, have students look at the following sentences, say each sentence out loud, substituting "it is" for each use of *its* or *it's*. They should be able to then determine which word to use.

1. It's my birthday.   (it is)

2. Its tail is too short.   (belonging to it)

3. No one knows its name.   (belonging to it)

4. It's time.   (it is)

5. I see that it's right.   (it is)

6. What is its purpose?   (belonging to it)

7. The cat chased its own tail.   (belonging to it)

8. It's time for its opening.   (it is; belonging to it)

9. I know that it's my turn.   (it is)

10. Its tire is flat.   (belonging to it)

Part IV: Commonly Confused Words

The following activity involves students using their knowledge of these commonly confused words in a paragraph.

Divide the class into two or three teams. Give ample time for each team to construct paragraphs that contain at least half of the words the class learned. Teams then read their paragraphs aloud, one sentence at a time, saying "blank" when a vocabulary word is to be inserted. If there are two teams, the first person on the other team to raise a hand can answer; if there are three teams, alternate between teams for answers. The answer should be spelled out for clarity, not just spoken. Then go to the next team for its paragraph. The team with the most correct answers wins. Some sentences that students construct might have more than one potential answer; as an example, a group might include a sentence such as, "Try not to _____ that." *Lose, affect,* and *alter* all fit the sentence, so the correct answer in most of these cases will depend on context.

Part V: Writing to Win

Chapter One: Active Voice

One activity that you can use for distinguishing between active and passive voice, besides simple rewriting, is to have students explain why the sentences work better in the active voice, or why they work better in the passive voice. Many sentences that were active will sound weak, silly, or awkward in passive voice. Students should recognize this, which will reemphasize differences between the two voices. Remind them that restructuring the passive sentences into active ones can work well, but revising, altering, or rewording their writing is another technique. They should have a feel for which type works best.

Here are two short paragraphs students can work on revising; they can complete the activity in pairs, if so desired. Note that the second version of each paragraph has been totally revised and reordered.

Paragraph A

In a new study by the Trekker Center for Social Research, it was found that women who support gun owners' rights report themselves to be happier in their relationships than women by whom gun *control* was supported. Eleven hundred women were interviewed by researcher Sally Gatillo over a period of about five years. They were asked to rate changes in their marital or relationship status and their overall happiness. When the data was examined, surprising results were found: The happiest women were the ones who owned many guns.

A new study by the Trekker Center for Social Research finds that women who support gun owners' rights report that they are happier in their relationships than women who support gun control. Researcher Sally Gatillo interviewed eleven hundred women over a period of about five years. She asked them to rate changes in their marital or relationship status and their overall happiness. When she examined the data, she found surprising results: The women who owned many guns were the happiest.

Paragraph B

Josquin Des Prez was a composer who wrote what are called motets. Most of the time, he is simply called "Josquin" by classical music listeners. Josquin worked during the Renaissance. A motet is a setting of a story taken from the Bible. It does not have to be used by the choir on a particular day in the church calendar, but it may be used at any point in the liturgy. Other musical pieces were also written by Des Prez. The most famous mass written by him is called the "Missa Pange Lingua." Later musicians were influenced by Josquin's ideas about composition.

The composer Josquin Des Prez worked during the Renaissance. Most of the time, classical music listeners call him "Josquin." Josquin wrote motets. A motet is a setting of a story from the Bible. A choir can use it at any point in the liturgy, rather than only on a particular day in the church calendar. Josquin also wrote other musical pieces; among the most famous is the "Missa Pange Lingua." Josquin's ideas about composition influenced later musicians.

For this activity, group students in the class into threes. One person will clearly and slowly state a fact in his or her own words. Most facts will have extraneous information and extra wording which students must eliminate in the initial paraphrase. The second team member needs to write down what the speaker says, verbatim. Then, the final person in the group will try to write a paraphrase of the second person's verbatim reiteration of the fact. They can then switch, so that each has the chance to take all three roles. Some students may see this as similar to the game "Whisper Down the Lane," in which information is distorted as it moves further from the source.

We have provided you with a list of facts that you can use for this activity:

- The first computer developed for personal use was called the Univac, which stands for Universal Automatic Computer. It was first used for the 1952 census.

- Only a small amount, less than 20 milligrams, of venom from the black mamba, an African snake, is sufficient to kill an adult.

- The one president who was elected and remained a bachelor while he was in office, was James Buchanan.

- Photography, before the invention of digital picture taking, involved the use of a chemical called silver nitrate, an enlarger, and water. It could take an hour to develop and print one picture.

- A single adult camel is able to drink up to 28 gallons of water at a time, but it is not stored in the animal's hump, as is commonly thought.

- Shakespeare wrote only 37 plays, and he is considered the greatest writer of English who ever lived.

- Water is the only substance we know of that expands when it freezes, which is why ice will float.

- The song, "White Christmas," was not written by a Christian. In fact, Irving Berlin, an American Jew, is the author.

- More species of insects exist than any other creature; over a million different kinds are known, but new types are discovered each year.

- World War II ended after the U.S. dropped an atomic bomb on the Japanese cities of Hiroshima and Nagasaki.

- A person who can jump three feet in the air, like a basketball player, could jump over 18 feet high on the Moon.

- The term "jiffy," often used in informal speech to mean "a short period of time," is actually a formal unit of time measurement in various scientific disciplines, including electronics, computing, and physics.

- Bananas are scientifically classified as berries, and the plants that produce them are not technically trees, but herbs. Unlike true trees, banana plants do not have woody stems.

- The tallest person to be documented through irrefutable evidence was Robert Wadlow, who grew to be 8 feet, 11.1 inches tall and weighed 490 pounds. Wadlow suffered from a pituitary condition that caused him to continue to grow after reaching adulthood.

- Despite his cruel treatment of fellow humans, Adolph Hitler was a vegetarian and an ardent supporter of animal rights. According to "Neugeist/Die Weisse Fahne," a German magazine, Hitler discouraged the consumption of meat "because of his general attitude toward life and his love for the world of animals."

- At birth, a person's eye has already reached its maximum size. The eye is the only organ in the human body that does not grow after birth.

- Joan of Arc was burned as a witch in 1431. Ironically, Pope Benedict XV canonized her as a saint in 1920 at St. Peter's Basilica in Rome.

- The tongue of an adult blue whale is roughly the same weight as the average adult male African elephant's entire body.

- More than 90% of all violent crimes are committed by someone who has eaten bread within the past 24 hours, and over 98% convicted felons eat bread on a regular basis.

- In a phenomenon known as the "photic sneeze reflex," people sneeze repeatedly when suddenly exposed to bright light. Aristotle wrote about the strange link between sneezing and sunlight in the fourth century B.C.

- The giant salvinia, a water fern native to South America, has become an invasive species in the United States. It forms large mats that can completely cover a body of water. A type of animal called a weevil that eats the fern can be used to control invasive salvinia.

- Fourth century Myra, Turkey, was home to a bishop who would eventually become famous around the world. He was Nicholas of Myra, a man known for his kindness to sailors, children, and poor people of all occupations. After his death, the saint was transformed into a hero of children. We know him as Santa Claus.

- The amount of money that a person must make in order to afford basic necessities (housing, food, transportation, medicine) is called a "living wage." The living wage differs from state to state because real estate prices, cost of transportation, and other factors vary.

- Richard Proenneke headed for Twin Lakes, Alaska, in the late 1960s. He became famous as the subject of the documentary called "Alone in the Wilderness," which shows him building his own log cabin, complete with a Dutch door and stone chimney; growing vegetables; hunting sheep and caribou, then, dressing and curing the meat in a smokehouse he built himself; and walking in snowshoes across the frozen lake in minus thirty-six degree weather.

- Samosas are fried pastries stuffed with potatoes, onions, peas, or cheese. They may also have a meat filling. A type of samosa is also part of the cuisine of Middle Eastern countries, Central Asian countries, and Portugal.

- The Miller in Chaucer's *Canterbury Tales* not only appears as a drunken bully, but also tells an obscene story. In the medieval period, millers had bad reputations. A miller was supposed to take, as his fee, a small portion of the grain that he milled, but some millers found ways to take more than their share.

- The poodle, although today considered a prissy, high-maintenance dog, was originally bred to retrieve birds that hunters shot out of the sky. Their fancily cut fur is only for show.

- Through the process of photosynthesis, plants use energy from the sun to convert carbon dioxide and water into sugars, such as sucrose and glucose, which gives them the energy to grow.

- Even though it is mistakenly believed that Victor Hugo's novel *Les Misérables* is set during the French Revolution, the novel opens in 1815, sixteen years after the Revolution and in the same year Napoleon was defeated at the Battle of Waterloo.

- Mario, the main character in Nintendo's Mario Brothers series, made his first appearance in the original Donkey Kong. However, in Donkey Kong, Mario was a carpenter instead of a plumber, and his name was Jumpman.

- Arabic numerals, the ten digits 0-9 that we use today, were invented by Indian mathematicians around 600 AD. Before that, there was no such thing as "zero."

- Morris Michtom created the first teddy bear in 1903. The toy is named after President Theodore Roosevelt, who, while on a hunting trip in Mississippi, refused to shoot a black bear cub that a fellow hunter captured and tied to a tree.

- Of the 206 bones in the body, 52 are located in the feet. However, there is a genetic abnormality that gives some people extra bones, referred to as "accessory ossicles," in each foot.

- Vlad Tepes, the inspiration for Bram Stoker's *Dracula*, is considered a national hero in Romania for defending the country against the Ottoman Turks. It is well known, however, that he did engage in torture.

- The first man to be launched into space was a Russian cosmonaut named Yuri Gagarin. When he returned to earth, he was an instantaneous hero in Russia, primarily because the event meant that the USA was losing the so-called "Space Race."

For this activity, we have supplied you with six groups of six to eight sentences each. The sentences are in random order, but they can be put together to make a coherent paragraph through the addition of transitional elements, combining, and some slight rewriting.

Divide the class into six groups and give each group one set of sentences to put in an order to construct a logical paragraph.

Repeat this process one more time so that each group revises two paragraphs. Select one member of a group to read that group's paragraph. Then, do the same for the second version. Have the students discuss the strengths of the paragraph they prefer. Repeat this until all the paragraphs have been dealt with.

A)   1.   Before Gutenberg's invention, all books were written by hand.

      2.   Johannes Gutenberg invented the idea of moveable type and a printing press, which made books affordable to nearly everyone.

      3.   Only the rich could afford books.

      4.   The first book ever printed by a machine was a copy of the Bible.

      5.   By 1599, over fifteen million books had been printed using his techniques.

      6.   Gutenberg never made any money from his invention.

      7.   It was printed in 1555, and two hundred copies were made.

Answers will vary. Possible version:

Johannes Gutenberg invented the idea of moveable type and a printing press, which made books affordable to nearly everyone. Before Gutenberg's invention, all books were written by hand, and only the rich could afford them. The first book ever produced by machine was a copy of the Bible. It was printed in 1555, and only two hundred copies of it were made. By 1599, though, over fifteen million books had been printed using Gutenberg's techniques. The famous inventor, however, never made any money from his invention.

B) 1. Whereas monks seek spiritual awareness through separation from the world, friars live among other people.

2. Neither monks nor friars are allowed to marry.

3. A monk is supposed to live a solitary life of prayer and religious contemplation.

4. Many people think that a monk and a friar perform the same job.

5. A friar is someone who lives among the poor and helps them, but has no earthly wealth for himself.

6. They are somewhat opposites.

7. Monks and friars do have some similarities.

Answers will vary. Possible version:

Many people think that a monk and a friar perform the same job; however, in many ways, they are opposites. Whereas monks seek spiritual awareness through separation from the world, friars live among other people. Another difference is that a monk is supposed to live a solitary life of prayer and religious contemplation. On the other hand, a friar is someone who lives among the poor and helps them, but has no earthly wealth for himself. Monks and friars do have one similarity, though: Neither one is allowed to marry.

C) 1. He seemed destined to represent his country in the Calgary Winter Olympics in 1988.

2. Reeves declared his intention to leave sports and focus on becoming an artist himself.

3. The speed skater Carl Reeves was a classic example of a natural athlete.

4. He was All-Canadian Champion in three skating events as a freshman at the University of Ottawa.

5. Everything changed after he attended an exhibition of the works of the abstract sculptor Ben Shamen.

6. As a child, he had excelled at hockey, distance running, and swimming.

Answers will vary. Possible version:

The speed skater Carl Reeves was a classic example of a natural athlete. As a child, he had excelled at hockey, distance running, and swimming. Reeves was also All-Canadian Champion in three skating events as a freshman at the University of Ottawa and seemed destined to represent his country in the Calgary Winter Olympics in 1988. Everything changed, however, after he attended an exhibition of the works of the abstract sculptor Ben Shamen. Reeves immediately declared his intention to leave sports and focus on becoming an artist himself.

D)
1. Alina seems prepared for any situation, doesn't get frustrated, keeps a smile on her face, and is pleasant to be around.

2. She and I have been friends for more than ten years, ever since elementary school.

3. I've always admired Alina for her confidence.

4. I am not.

5. That was when a drunk driver smashed into her car.

6. Only once did I see her angry.

7. Lots of my friends are jealous of Alina.

Answers will vary. Possible version:

Alina seems prepared for any situation, doesn't get frustrated, keeps a smile on her face, and is pleasant to be around. Although lots of my friends are jealous of Alina, I am not. In fact, I've always admired her for her confidence. She and I have been friends for more than ten years, ever since elementary school. Only once did I see her angry, and that was when a drunk driver smashed into her car.

E) 1. Decorating the tree is one of her favorite activities.

2. We sometimes spend the whole day picking out a tree.

3. All the ornaments have stories behind them.

4. She puts each piece of tinsel on the tree individually.

5. They are all the same and I hear them each year.

6. My mom just adores Christmas.

7. What a waste of time!

8. Halloween appeals to me because I can almost become another person for a night.

Answers will vary. Possible version:

Halloween appeals to me because I can almost become another person for a night, but my mom just adores Christmas. Sometimes, we spend the whole day picking out a tree, which to me is a waste of time! Decorating the tree is one of her favorite activities. She puts each piece of tinsel on the tree individually, and all the ornaments have stories behind them. They are all the same and I hear them each year.

F) 1. The town of Pisa, Italy, was in the middle of a series of wars with neighboring states.

2. Construction was delayed for almost a hundred years.

3. The soil settled, allowing the tower to remain somewhat upright.

4. If construction had continued, the tower would have fallen.

5. In August, 1173, construction began on the bell tower of a cathedral in the town.

6. The tower began to lean; it was built on poor soil.

7. The Leaning Tower of Pisa is among Italy's major tourist attractions.

Answers will vary. Possible version:

The town of Pisa, Italy, was in the middle of a series of wars with neighboring states. Despite this, in August, 1173, construction began on the bell tower of a cathedral in the town. The tower, however, began to lean; it was built on poor soil. Construction was delayed for almost a hundred years because, if it had continued, the tower would have fallen.

The soil then settled, allowing the tower to remain upright, but tilted. Today, the Leaning Tower of Pisa is among Italy's major tourist attractions.

For this next transition activity, you should display or hand out to the class the following passages, which have blanks where the transitions should be. The type of transition called for is listed in the blank.

The activity could also work by dividing the class into groups. The blanks are labeled to determine what type of transition is asked for. As each blank is encountered, the class will decide which transitions can work well in the blanks and which one fits best. Sometimes, there may be debate, and the class can then decide on the preferred transition.

Paragraph A

Place, U.S. Soldiers and Iraqi citizens tore down a large statue of Saddam Hussein. In addition, ordinary people, who had hated the dictator, began to celebrate. Pronoun took off their shoes In Addition began to hit the Repeated Word with Pronoun. Many Westerners did not understand what was happening Contrast. Time Order, television reporters began to explain that this type of behavior is common in many Middle Eastern countries. Pronoun is one of the worst insults possible. Repeated Word were showing Pronoun extreme disgust. Contrast, this was a happy time, In Addition. Repeated Word was Time Order gone. Place, sirens were wailing with joy, people were shooting into the air in celebration, Contrast the Army still had a great deal to do Time Order Baghdad could be made safe.

Answers will vary. Accept any that help the paragraph and fit the type that is requested in the blank.

In Baghdad, U.S. Soldiers and Iraqi citizens tore down a large statue of Saddam Hussein. In addition, ordinary people, who had hated the dictator, began to celebrate. They took off their shoes and began to hit the statue with them. Many Westerners did not understand what was happening, though. Soon, television reporters began to explain that this type of behavior is common in many Middle Eastern countries: It is one of the worst insults possible. Citizens were showing their extreme disgust. Nevertheless, this was a happy time, too. Saddam Hussein was finally gone. Nearby, sirens were wailing with joy, people were shooting into the air in celebration, but the Army still had a great deal to do before Baghdad could be made safe.

Paragraph B

<u>Time Order</u>, we review the company's financial status, goals, <u>In Addition</u> other factors to determine <u>Pronoun</u> budget for the coming year. <u>Contrast</u>, the country is experiencing a severe economic crisis <u>Time Order</u> that has affected all types of businesses. In consideration of the effect the <u>Repeated Idea</u> is having on city budgets, <u>In Addition</u> <u>In Addition</u> to our company, we must lower operating expenses. <u>Effect</u>, we will be using <u>Pronoun</u> own staff to produce materials that <u>Repeated Idea</u> has traditionally sent to factories in Canada. <u>Effect</u>, we will no longer be able to offer you any additional work <u>Time Order</u>.

<u>In December</u>, we review the company's financial status, goals, <u>and</u> other factors to determine <u>our</u> budget for the coming year. <u>However</u>, the country is experiencing a severe economic crisis <u>presently</u> that has affected all types of businesses. In consideration of the effect the <u>economy</u> is having on city budgets, <u>and</u> <u>also</u> to our company, we must lower operating expenses. <u>Consequently</u>, we will be using <u>our</u> own staff to produce materials that <u>the business</u> has traditionally sent to factories in Canada. <u>Therefore</u>, we will no longer be able to offer you any additional work <u>next year</u>.

Paragraph C

<u>Time Order</u>, people hear the word "prairie," <u>In Addition</u> they think of "shortgrass" prairies, like the <u>Repeated Word</u> that make up the Great Plains. In parts of the country, <u>Contrast</u>, another kind of prairie once flourished. <u>Pronoun</u> was called a "tallgrass prairie." Several features of this ecosystem made it vitally important to American history. <u>Example</u>, there was the close relationship between the grass <u>In Addition</u> the grazing animals <u>Pronoun</u> supported. Prairie cultures, <u>Example</u>, planned their lives around the movements of the bison. <u>In Addition</u>, there was the structure of the tallgrass: The most important parts of the plants grew and decomposed underground. <u>Time Order</u>, the decomposed matter formed a very rich topsoil. <u>Effect</u>, it was ideal for planting crops. <u>Time Order</u>, ninety-nine percent of the tallgrass prairies has been converted to farmland.

<u>Today</u>, people hear the word "prairie," <u>and</u> they think of "shortgrass" prairies, like the <u>prairies</u> that make up the Great Plains. In parts of the country, <u>however</u>, another kind of prairie once flourished. <u>It</u> was called a "tallgrass prairie." Several features of this ecosystem made it vitally important to American history. <u>For example</u>, there was the close relationship between the grass <u>and</u> the grazing animals prairie grass supported. Prairie cultures, <u>for instance</u>, planned their lives around the movements of the bison. <u>In addition</u>, there was the structure of the tallgrass: The most important parts of the plants grew and decomposed underground. <u>Then</u>, the decomposed matter formed a very rich topsoil. <u>Consequently</u>, it was ideal for planting crops. <u>Eventually</u>, ninety-nine percent of the tallgrass prairies has been converted to farmland.